CONTENTS

THE
LIGHTHOUSE
KEEPER

THE
LIGHTHOUSE
KEEPER

A Story of Mind Mastery

DAVID RICHARDS

ISBN: 978-1-09830-145-3

For my mother Donna, who always believed in me.

PROLOGUE

A rooster's crow broke the pre-dawn silence. William the Conqueror. That was the name his father had given the fine black Australorp that ruled their roost. He was a head taller than their remaining eight roosters, with darts of tan and brown the only color in his otherwise ebony cape. His crowing was distinct in that it ended suddenly, as if something had caught in the rooster's throat. He crowed again. It was soon followed by a gaggle of impatient, agitated clucking. Then nothing. The rooster crowed again. More clucking. Somewhere further away, another rooster crowed its shrill reply.

In the next room, heavy feet found their way onto the floor. The feet shuffled a short distance before there was again a brief silence. The silence broke with the sound of one boot and then a second, scraping over the floor as they were put on and laced. The footfalls resumed heavier now, louder, moving with alertness and purpose.

He hated the sound of the creaking door. Yet it always came. Day after day, after day. And, he feared, always would come. The rest of his life, the door would creak. Maybe he could oil its hinges for some quiet. And for a time, it would silence the door. But that was only quieting an otherwise unsettling truth.

He'd been awake at least twenty minutes, grateful he hadn't yet heard it and looking for some last morsel of sleep to appease his restful hunger, bitter that the creak would inevitably come. And now, as these heavy boots plodded closer, he felt his pulse race. His imagination, as it so often did when he woke early, raced with it. The door was going to open and it wasn't going to be who he expected. No.

It would be Death. Death, and not a faceless apparition shrouded in a black cloak with a scythe. His Death would be covered in chicken filth, with maggots worming their way down what was left of a ragged, torn face. It would have the face of some rotting rooster; the comb tattered and scarred like the dead sail of a lifeless ship. The eyes black, the black of some infinite foreboding darkness and the beak a hooked, unnatural thing, with wattles that sagged in shredded streams of decaying flesh. He clenched his teeth as the footsteps stopped immediately outside his door. The latch clicked. The door groaned its agonizing note as it opened.

"Sam, time to rise," his father said in a calm, steady tone. His voice was deep, and the words were heavy, like the sound of stone slabs scraping against one another. Without waiting for a reply, his father turned and made his way to the kitchen.

Sam Seagrim sat up in his bed, as much to show his father that he was in fact awake as to get himself moving to start the day. He ran a hand through his sandy blond hair then rubbed his eyes and looked outside. A bright moon hung just beneath the tree tops, piercing the night with vibrant blue beams. The rooster crowed again.

"Alright." He said, waving a hand in the empty air and pushing himself off the bed.

Breakfast passed with little said between father and son. It was routine. His father cooked: the eggs, the bacon, the toast. Sam fetched the jam and the milk which, on some occasions when the seasons permitted, would be substituted with freshly squeezed orange juice.

As quickly as the food was ready, it was eaten. Sam washed the dishes and left them in the drying rack while his father brought in more wood for the fire. All the while, a chorus of rooster cries played in the background, a nagging reminder of the day's activities.

With the sun just beginning to paint the eastern sky in soft oranges and pinks, they were outside; he would collect eggs while his father walked the fence line. The integrity of the fence confirmed, the chickens would be freed from the coop to roam and feed.

They had just over two hundred birds divided into four chicken houses. The count had been higher, but they'd lost a dozen due to a sickness that had hit the coop early in the summer. A fox had breached the perimeter and gotten one more, but not before William the Conqueror made the sly trickster pay a heavy price. Sam had gotten to the coop first. There were feathers everywhere, even some still floating in the air. William had picked up an awkward limp, and clawed at the ground in obvious irritation. Upon closer inspection, Sam saw that the remains of one of the fox's eyes was snagged on William's foot.

Even with the losses, it was the largest chicken farm in the county by a good eighty chickens and they made a comfortable living. Most of their hens averaged around ninety eggs a year; as the cooler months came on, they'd select three dozen or so of the younger hens to sell at the market for meat. Egg production always died off in the winter months; his father would take odd jobs around town to subsidize their income. Soon he knew, his father would tell him to do the same.

The coops smelled of straw and crap, a stench that was never quite ordinary, despite the mundane tasks associated with it. The smell was aggravated by the poor ventilation and, in the warmer months, the remains of the previous day's baking heat.

The chickens' frenzied exit had kicked up a thick dust, which hung in the air, sticking to him and filling his nostrils. Their curious clucks to greet the day were met by the chirping of the chicks, which were kept in a separate, smaller coop a few feet away from the main chicken-house surrounded by wire mesh and given feed to ensure their growth wasn't left to chance.

The eggs collected and stored inside the house, Sam went to cleaning the coops. He swept the poop into a dustbin and from there into a small pail he carried with him. He moved mechanically and with the ease built of habit, the tasks a part of him now, the product of having done them almost daily for the better part of four years.

He paused, setting the pail on the top shelf in the main coop and looked at his father. The older Seagrim, having completed the perimeter walk, turned his attention to chopping wood on the side of the house, a chore he preferred to do before the sun was above the trees. That errand complete, he would take the morning's supply of eggs into town to sell. That left Sam to gather the chopped wood and stack it, taking enough into the house to keep the stove fire burning for the day. That left laundry that needed to be taken down to the creek to be washed, brought back, and hung to dry.

He would make lunch, eat, then clean the house. As the sun burned its arc across the sky, he would have an hour or two to himself. In the past, he might have gone to the Flannery house, ten minutes' walk across farmland and pasture to see his friend Sean. But the youngest Flannery would be joining his two older brothers at university. He had other friends, further away in both distance and association. Some, like Sean, would be headed to school. Others found themselves treading on similar ground as he; angling themselves into the family business.

He loved his father; they'd grown closer in the years since his mother had died. He'd briefly explored the idea that his father would remarry. It wouldn't have sat well with him and he was ready to protest though the subject never came up in conversation and, after two years, seemed less and less likely with each passing month as his father found solace at home, and in the company of his only son.

Instead, his father threw himself into work. Errands and odd jobs around the home-front that had languished for months, years even, were addressed. One day the roof leaked, the next day it didn't. There was a draft from a poorly sealed window, and then there wasn't. With methodical precision, his father tackled tasks that had stacked up like unkempt cords of wood, until they were all neatly addressed.

After that, he turned his attention to their family business; within a year they'd doubled the number of chickens they had.

None of this was lost on Sam. And he sensed the tug no, the burden, of taking over the family business encroaching on the fabric of his life. Had felt it, even tasted it in the air. Maybe it had always been there.

He withdrew a game from his back pocket. It was a simple stick, with a small cup attached to one end. On the other end, a long thin rope connected to a wooden ball; the object was to get the ball into the cup. He'd picked it up a few months back when the circus rolled through town. He looped the ball upward and managed to bounce it off the cup rim. He tried again. Success. He'd made a game within the game, seeing how many consecutive times he could land the ball inside the cup. His high score was twenty-seven, but he hadn't been spending much time on it.

The ball caught the attention of William the Conqueror, who had wandered back into the coop, vigilantly patrolling his domain. He paused, eyeing Sam and his little game before bobbing and strutting to the coop's top shelf. As roosters go, he moved stealthily, quietly clucking under his breath as he carefully walked closer to Sam, who was lost in the game.

When he had drawn close enough, William struck, reaching out for the ball. The commotion surprised Sam, who dropped the cup game on the floor.

"William, you idiot." Sam exclaimed, bending down to pick up the game.

William too was agitated, fanning his wings and hopping back. As he did so, he knocked against the pail. It rocked from one side to the other, but instead of finding the edge of the shelf, found only open air, and fell. The pail crashed on top of Sam, spilling its contents.

He stood, covered in feces, urine, and straw, his face a red mask of anger.

His father was late getting back from town, but having sold all the eggs, called the day a success. Sam had spent the afternoon finishing his chores and then stayed outside, drawing trees and birds, and occasionally pulling out his ball-cup game. Now, as they ate, Sam wrestled with his thoughts.

"Something on your mind?" his father asked in between bites of food.

Sam pushed his fork around his plate, plowing indifferently through his mashed potatoes. Before he spoke, he felt the tremble in his throat rise. "I don't want this."

"It's what's for supper."

Sam pushed his plate away from him. "No, not this. I want to leave. Leave here. Find my own way."

His father stopped eating and set his fork on the plate. "What about the farm? I need you here."

"But you don't need me. You just need a body. You can find someone local to help out." It was a truth, neither damning nor invigorating, but like a truth once spoken, it couldn't be taken back. A spider of panic scurried up his spine. He looked at his father, assessing whether or not the words had delivered a sting.

Sam's father wiped his mouth with his napkin and pushed back from the table. His tongue made a circle behind closed lips, tasting the words, ingesting them. He stood and walked to the window looking out on the chicken houses. When he spoke again, his voice was soft. Soft, as gravel goes. Soft in a way that reminded Sam of when his mother died, but now that voice lacked the fragility, the weakness, that he had heard back then.

"I'm surprised it's taken you this long." His father said, without turning back to look at him. "I figured you'd have gotten sick of this place two seasons ago. Was surprised when you stayed on. Happy of course, but surprised."

Sam looked at his father, then looked away. He had been wanting to leave. Had played out the conversation in his head so many times, but always met resistance. His reasoning always fell flat, in the best cases, met with bitter anger, and in the worst cases, with the searing brand of shame. Like there was some invisible barrier he always ran into that kept him silent. And now the words having come out he found...there was no barrier at all.

"What will you do?" His father continued, his eyes fixed on something in the yard. Or perhaps not fixed on anything at all.

Sam started to speak then cleared his throat. "I know there isn't enough money for me to attend university. I- I thought I would head to the coast."

"To be a fisherman?" His father turned, unable to restrain the blossom of surprise across his brow. "That's a hard life."

"No," Sam stood up now, "I don't want to fish. I want to go to the lighthouse at Black Eagle."

As quickly as the surprise appeared, it was gone. In its place, a flash of something rippled across his father's brow. Was it disappointment?

"Sam," his voice had lost its softness, "that man...what have you heard about him?"

"The keeper? Sean's older brother worked under him. He's working Hook Head now. Will probably be the head keeper in a few years. He's engaged to be married."

"What do you want Sam?"

Sam couldn't stop the words from coming. "I don't know. I know I don't want this. I want to find my own way."

Sam's father sighed. He sat down in a heap and reached for a water, finishing it in one giant gulp.

"Alright. Let me see what I can do."

PART ONE

KEEPER OF THE LIGHT

CHAPTER ONE
THE APPRENTICE

Black Eagle Lighthouse sat atop a small cropping of rock a few meters above sea level. It reached up from the ocean floor like a hand, the dark, jagged appendage of some earthly celestial, its fingers spread wide, the fingertips disappearing into the sea on the island's eastern side. The waves made splintered assaults into the grooves between the fingers, crashing against the rocks in their ceaseless assault. On occasion, reached more than half the lighthouse's height.

On the back of the hand sat Black Eagle Lighthouse. Slightly less than fifty meters high, it was painted in equal thirds of navy blue, white, and navy blue again before surrendering to the catwalk and lantern. A single door on the southern side supplied entrance to the lighthouse, which could be accessed by way of a small dock on the leeward side to the west. Once docked, one followed steps which had been dutifully carved out of the rock as they meandered their way up to the entryway.

A few miles to the west, the faint glow of the mainland and the nearest town beckoned in the greying day. It was dusk. Save for the flickering, distant lights from the town, there was ocean as far as the eye could see.

A small boat navigated the agitated waters and headed west into the waking night, making its way towards the lighthouse. The boat carved a purposeful path, cutting through the waves and spraying their remnants across the bow, drenching the crew in the process.

Dark, pregnant clouds murmured overhead, flashing alarm in stuttering bouts, illuminating the boat's crew, who sensed they were racing the storm clouds to their destination. They worked with seasoned precision in the familiar waters. The boat's captain held steady on the course, even as the boat strained against the strengthening storm. She would deliver the day's goods and have her crew safely home in time for a late dinner.

The cargo they ferried was of the standard fare: dried foods and a few frozen steaks...a treat for the lighthouse keeper. There were two weeks' worth of fresh fruit; there was milk and cheese, and some bars of chocolate. They carried with them a cord of wood for the lighthouse fireplace. The captain knew the keeper had rain barrels, but had brought a few gallons of fresh water for good measure.

There were newspapers and magazines from the previous weeks, and enough toiletries to last a month. There were other odds and ends, including empty trash cans, which the crew would exchange with the lighthouse keeper for his full ones. There was all this, and something the captain brought only rarely on previous trips; a passenger.

The passenger hadn't said much, this young Seagrim fellow. Hadn't brought much for that matter, though the captain didn't know for how long her passenger planned on staying at the lighthouse. Or how long the keeper would let him stay.

She knew precious little about her passenger. He was medium height, with shoulders that drooped slightly. Curls of blond hair escaped from underneath his red watch-cap and his face was clean-shaven, if he had a need to shave at all. She didn't think he would fare well at sea... not without some more meat on his bones. An older man had accompanied him to the dock, but had not hesitated to turn and leave as the younger man boarded the vessel. They hugged, and with a swift, firm pat on the back, the older man was gone. As the apprentice boarded, he tipped his cap and said, in a voice not yet bereft of youth, "I am the lighthouse keeper's apprentice." It was an excessively stuffy and inflated introduction, and she popped it out of the air with a vigorous handshake. She noted his hands were slightly calloused, enough so that she quietly reassessed him and his seaworthiness.

She introduced herself as Captain Stenson, to which Seagrim inquired if there might be a spot for him below-deck so as to keep out of the way of the crew. He politely refused her offer to assist with his duffel bag, which even now threatened to topple him onto one side. She took him to the small room next to her quarters. The room was lit with a kerosene lamp, which swayed with the ocean's mood. Seagrim threw his duffel bag and smaller bag down on one of the room's two benches and sat down next to them. They exchanged smiles and she closed the door behind her.

Stranger still, the captain had only come to know about Sam Seagrim thanks to the lighthouse keeper. The previous month, her crew was short two men, both out sick. She'd left the wheelhouse, and the tedium of completing her log book, while they were docked at Black Eagle to assist in ferrying supplies into the lighthouse storage room. The lighthouse smelled of wet stone and electricity, the combination of which created a sense of alarm. There were dank, dark places within the lighthouse that never saw the sun. The generator hummed its constant note while the waves crashed against the windward side of the tiny island. For the discomfort the place emanated, the generator sound was entrancing which, in turn, only exacerbated the feeling of unease. Outside, there was the crescendo of wave smashing into rock, followed immediately by the wave remnants raining down on the side of the lighthouse and surrounding walkway. She wanted to find it peaceful, but could only manage depressing. How did someone find peace in this kind of life, she wondered. Inside the lighthouse, the ocean sounds bounced off the walls in large, vacant echoes. Somewhere inside the lower level of the lighthouse, there was the steady sound of water dripping. The store room was on the third floor, and she left the boxes she hauled at the base of the stairs for one of her crew to carry the rest of the way.

On her final run from the boat, the keeper had gently grabbed her arm and told her that the apprentice would be at the docks with the next month's supply run, and that he would be grateful to the captain for bringing the young man safely to Black Eagle.

Armand was something of a hermit, she surmised. She couldn't remember the last time he'd been seen in town; four months at least. When it happened, the news raced through the shops and bars faster than a sprinting jack rabbit fleeing a hound. If he struck up conversation, it was never more than a few words, a handful of head nods, and a sincere, deep smile that Stenson thought might contain the slightest trace of madness. He was present, but utterly detached from what was happening around him, she thought. People never referred to him by name; it was always "the keeper" or for those who liked a little drama, "the keeper of Black Eagle", as if it was a title bestowed upon him for some noteworthy cause by the unseen royalty of the deep. Some of the older people from the coast called him a wickie, but as long as she'd known of him, Black Eagle had run on electricity.

His entrance into a tavern was enough to quiet the crowd until he made his way to the bar and ordered his usual; a glass of water. She had discovered his name by accident. "Armand" was scribbled on a parcel she'd once delivered years ago. The first time she called him by his name, he seemed surprised at hearing it.

He must lead a hollow, barren life, she thought. Alone, on purpose. By choice. Other captains had mused that lighthouse keepers were a tranquil lot, especially now that most lighthouses had moved away from oil lamps, which were labor intensive and called for multiple keepers per house. These speculations were issued side by side with stories of catches of fish too big to haul, mermaids, and other maritime tales.

As these captains saw it, the rhythmic, enchanting sound of the waves, broken occasionally by a gull or, on rare instances, a humpback, must be nature's tonic for the drudgery of a landlocked existence. For the keeper, gone were the days of wicks and fuel, gone too, the need for teams of men to man the houses. All that solitude, the present thinking went, what could be better other than being captain of a ship which, of course, they agreed was the height of good fortune.

Captain Stenson didn't share their sentiment. She loved her life and enjoyed her privacy, but reveled in the moments, both good and bad, with her crew. What was life without friends, without family? *Hollow*, the word came back to her. *Hollow like the echo of waves inside a lighthouse.* Armand had a rowboat moored to the dock, but Stenson sensed every time she made the supply run that the little boat hadn't been used at all in the time since her last visit. Who would he visit? At best, it was good for fishing away from the island. If it were needed to get back to town in case of an emergency, the journey alone would be precarious and fraught with peril if the sea were angry.

Seagrim stayed below decks astern, duffel bag and knapsack alongside him, book opened and held a few inches from his face. He kept his red cap on. In the lamp light, she could better see his brown eyes, pudgy nose, and just how young he looked.

Shortly before they left town, supplies loaded, she had gone down to check on him. He had been playing some inane game with a ball on a string, trying to catch the ball in a little wooden cup. It was the kind of trinket one picked up at the fair. He declined her offer of water, the grey peacoat he wore nearly swallowing him up. She checked on him again at the midpoint of their journey. He been playing the game again, quickly set it aside when she opened the cabin door, and reached for a book laid face-down on the table in front of him. She noted the book was *The Lighthouse at the End of the World* by Jules Verne.

She thought of checking again, more for her own

benefit she realized, and decided against it. He was odd, but otherwise harmless. Twice had been enough; he likely didn't need anything, and had declined anything she'd offered anyway.

In the distance, the lantern of Black Eagle's dock danced in the blustery wind and through the growing haze of dark, Stenson soon made out the shape of the landing. White water sprayed across the tiny island as waves pummeled the far side with their relentless ferocity. The storm was moving in, faster than she'd reckoned. She estimated the waves were exploding up the side of the lighthouse as high as seven meters. If they were still unloading when the waves reached ten meters, getting home would be a white-knuckle adventure unto itself. She eased the boat's throttle and deftly guided the boat alongside the dock.

Below deck, Sam was getting deeper into his book. At least, that's what he told himself. He would read for a bit, then pull out his game and attempt to break his current record of seventy-one catches in a row. He got close, only six shy of breaking the mark, but the shipped pitched forward as the bow dropped slightly into a trough, and he missed the ball. This latest attempt having failed, he put the game down and returned to the book.

He had grown fond of the main character, Vazquez, but mourned the loss of his fellow lighthouse keepers, Felipe and Moriz. He briefly imagined himself as Vazquez, and felt the blossom of anger open in reaction to the villainous pirate leader Kongre, who clearly had no redeeming qualities whatsoever. Coming back to himself, he hoped by the book's end that the scoundrel would meet his fate.

Sam's father had given him the book, something to read on his journey. He enjoyed reading, almost always enjoyed books about the sea, and hadn't previously heard of this one. He shifted positions on the bench, and his book marker fell to the floor. It was a faded picture of his mother, who had died many years prior. He reached down to retrieve the photo and paused.

She had been so young, and he early in his schooling at the time of her passing. Her long, dark hair swirled in healthy waves around her head, and the vivacity in her smile and brilliance in her eyes made him feel like she might leap from the photo into the tiny cabin where he sat. A tear fell onto the picture.

Sam sat back and wiped his eyes. Images of her and fragments of her voice flashed across his mind. The adventure and excitement he'd felt when he'd first set foot aboard the boat...*El Viaje*, he thought it was called...were suddenly lost in a swirl of angst and sorrow. The lamp light flickered, the storm outside intensified.

He came across a memory of a spring day. The air

was alive with the triumphant chirps of birds as small pink flowers danced in the air like tiny fairies. He smelled honeysuckle on the breeze. He was five, maybe six. There was the gurgling sound of water and the shushing of a stronger wind through the tree tops. A stream. Not far from their home. His father, still in his work pants with a hat tipped back on his head, casually minding a fishing rod at the water's edge. He sat next to his father, marveling at a dandelion. His father patting him on the head to get his attention. Looking up, Sam followed his father's hand to a yellow, orange, and black-ringed snake slipping out of the water onto the stream's far side.

Laughter. Her voice. His mind's eye turned, *yearned*. Focused.

There she was. She wore a pretty blue dress. Her hair caught the sunlight, and her skin shone a golden hue. She was calming the end of a picnic blanket that had been excited by the breeze.

His father turned. Said something. He couldn't remember what it was, but felt the awe in his father's baritone voice. Like the commanding calm of a lion's low growl. Sam's gaze remained fixed on his mother, who pulled back slightly, as if what his father had said had affected her physically. Her cheeks reddened and her smile deepened. In that moment, he thought he knew what his mother must have been like as a little girl. Sweet. Shy. Charming and playful.

Her brilliant blue eyes shifted their gaze from his father to him. The spark in her eyes caught a different kind of fire. Her face softened gracefully, the way clouds soften sunlight. Her eyes grew bigger. He didn't understand the look at the time, not in any comprehensible way he could articulate, but now saw it plainly. It was hope. Adoration. Joy. It was the look of love, the kind of look that is somehow reserved for mothers and their children.

Sam heard his own voice, a foreign and tiny thing, calling to her in words he couldn't make out. She laughed and nodded her head, then motioned for him to join her. He sprung up with an eager smoothness that surprised him. He was conscious of how close to the ground he was; he saw himself as a dragonfly, moving just above the blades of the tall, swaying grasses.

He closed the distance between them as she pulled on a bunch of grapes. She extended her hand and he gingerly plucked one from its pedicle. She ran a hand through his hair and pulled him close to her. He felt all the warmth, safety, and tenderness of a mother's embrace. Could smell her perfume. It was a sublime space of happiness.

That happiness was ripped away by the wailing boat horn, indicating their approach to Black Eagle.

Sam wiped his eyes, now wet with tears. He returned the photograph to the book and shoved it into his knapsack. He wasn't about to let the captain or any of her crew see him like this; he dried his eyes thoroughly against his coat. This wouldn't be a great first impression for the lighthouse keeper either, a voice in his head warned. He slung his knapsack over one shoulder, dragged the duffel bag with his free hand, and headed topside.

The wind had picked up considerably and the sky erupted in spasmodic sparks of lightning as the storm labored overhead. A sideways, spitting rain was coming in from the west. White water hissed down on them in cold sheets. The boat, now docked, rocked in restrained unease in the choppy waters, like a toddler waddling in an oversized winter coat teeters over uneven ground.

The crew was methodically moving supplies off the boat in a loose daisy chain, with several men ferrying supplies up from the storage and handing them over to carriers on the dock, who then took the stores up the steps. At the top of the steps, there in the doorway, the imposing silhouette of the lighthouse keeper stepped to the side to allow men to pass.

CHAPTER TWO
BLACK EAGLE

Sleep's warm embrace proved elusive the first night in Black Eagle Lighthouse.

It wasn't simply the matter of spending the night away from the familiarity and comfort of home; he'd mentally prepared himself for that. Sam had been away from home before. He'd gone camping and found, much to his delight, once he became so thoroughly exhausted, he could sleep anywhere. Against a tree, no matter how rough or unaccommodating the roots underneath him might be. On a boulder even, provided he had something on which to rest his head.

Nor was he afraid of a little solitude. In school, he enjoyed time to himself. While the other boys tackled athletic pursuits, he wrote. He wrote poems, or stories of faraway, imagined lands with mystical creatures and people. Sometimes he wrote letters to different people in his life. One day, a note to his father. The next, a teacher. The day after that, a girl in class he liked. He never delivered the letters, but writing them made him feel better in some strange, unexplored way. He told himself it didn't matter, and found an odd comfort in that. When he ran out of words, he turned to drawing pictures. These too he never shared with anyone, but they adorned the walls of his bedroom like errant pieces of wallpaper. Moreover, at the lighthouse, he wasn't alone.

True, the lighthouse keeper...Armand, he had introduced himself as...was there. But what to make of him. He was tall. Too tall it seemed for the cramped quarters of Black Eagle; it wasn't as though he had to hunch over, or crane his neck down to fit into spaces. It was like the ceilings, even the walls, pulled back a bit to make room for him. It was a strange sensation, and an unsettling one at that.

The elixir of sea and sun had weathered and aged his host; Sam guessed the old man might be sixty, but looked two decades older. Armand wasn't gaunt, but was the kind of lean Sam imagined came from living the austere and, he now feared, barren life of a lighthouse keeper. His shoulders were strong and still broad, his hands rough with real work and age. His angular nose dipped down onto thick white, neatly-kept facial hair, which subsided into cheeks that were only now starting to lose their fullness. His eyes, hazel Sam guessed in the low light, were insightful and peering, ripe with intelligence.

Armand hadn't said much that first night. When he spoke, it was one or two-word sentences. His voice was throaty and contained none of the frailty Sam would have associated with someone who looked as old as Armand. If Armand had had any conversations with the ship's crew, Sam hadn't heard any of them. They had all gone back aboard the Viaje and departed for home, nary a word having been exchanged between suppliers and supplied.

His host was constantly in motion. "Welcome" in that deep voice that echoed off the walls of each room. With the wave of one hand, Armand opened his home to Sam. He turned and started up the thin, rusting spiral staircase that served as the spine of the house. "Sleep here" as the ragged wooden door creaked open to Sam's room. A twin bed stuck out from the back of the room, flanked on either side by small cubby holes with two-foot tall center bar windows in their middle. The room smelled of old books, though he saw none present. The bed looked big, but Sam reasoned it was because the room was so narrow, with barely enough space to maneuver along the bedsides. A small, elevated platform near the foot of the bed on the left side held a small dresser; behind it, a small door that blended evenly with the wall, save for a small, brass knob. A pair of small wooden buckets sat on the floor at the foot of the bed. On the right, a little round table and accompanying chair might serve as a desk. On it sat a small plate of meat, green beans, and potatoes, accompanied by a wooden cup filled with water.

"Dinner."

Up by the headboard on the left-hand side, a nightstand had been crammed in between the bed and the white wall, just underneath the cubby. A light on the nightstand flickered in response to a concussion of thunder.

"Sleep well." And with that, Armand closed the door, his heavy footfalls lessening in volume as he climbed the stairs.

The meal was decent enough, but then again, Sam had been hungry. He had little sense of time and knew only that it had darkened early with the storm's arrival. He felt it was too early to turn in, and wrestled with the idea of exploring. Would Armand be upset? He opted instead to open his journal.

BLACK EAGLE, DAY 1

Well, I'm here. The boat ride wasn't as bad as I thought it would be. The seas were rough, and the boat seemed tossed about on the waves, but no one showed any alarm, so I didn't either. I didn't really talk with the crew. I heard them chatting and singing as they worked...they didn't seem at all bothered by the tempest swirling around us! The captain was nice enough, though I don't remember her name.

I don't care what he says, I know father is disappointed. At the dock, there was no hiding that look on his face. I can't help but feel he'll be happy though, knowing that I've taken up his suggestion to write of my experiences so that I can capture my time here and reflect on it at a later date.

Armand is odd. And this storm scares me. It's so very different from a storm in the country.

At that moment, a flash of lightning lit up the night and the crack of thunder followed immediately after. The nightstand light flickered again, more severely, as if the generator had been dealt a staggering blow. It paused in its dim state, and he thought it might actually die. But it flickered again, then strengthened, then was as bright as it had been a moment before. He set down his pencil, stepped away from the desk and was on the bed in a heap, wooden game in hand. He was determined to break his record and, a voice in the back of his mind suggested, to take his mind off the storm. It was a voice he knew well. It was the voice of the shape he felt crouched next to him sometimes, when he was sitting in a chair, or in his bed. He could never make out the shape clearly, but knew it had wide eyes that darted from one spot to the next. It was the voice that whispered to him all the terrible things that might happen to him. It was the voice of Fear.

He focused on how well he had done playing the game on the boat, and how the swaying of the boat had actually been a benefit, honing is wooden ball-catching skills. After six failed attempts, he blew past his old record and made it all the way up to ninety-six. He was elated, and eager to crack the one hundred-catch mark.

His elation quickly subsided, and he swapped out the game with his book, reading to the end of the current chapter before setting the book down.

By then the storm was alive and unleashing its gathering fury on the tiny island, with the night just three hours underway. The book was good, intriguing even, but he was exhausted. Between the boat ride and actually being here, his mind was ready to shut down. He was committed to writing in his journal every night, and felt good that he had managed a few lines. Sleep, he thought, would come easily enough. He turned off the light and searched for sleep, but it would not come. The storm, it seemed, had restless intentions.

After several fruitless minutes, the light on the nightstand was back on, the contents of his knapsack spilled onto the bed in a jumble. There was another book, C.S. Forester's *Mr. Midshipman Hornblower*, his sketch pad, a few pencils, and several manuals on lighthouses. He wasn't sure why he brought them; he knew their contents thoroughly, and felt certain mastery of the lighthouse would come in short order. There just wasn't much to it. If something needed painting, he would paint it. If a window broke, he would replace it. Clean the lens. Clean the chimney. There was a logbook to be maintained. In it, he would track weather patterns, note the time of day the light was turned on and off, and record any incidents. Maybe taking care of the generator would be something new for him; he hadn't worked with one back on the farm. He was eager to prove his worth, and wondered how soon it would be before he was ready to run a lighthouse of his own.

The way he saw it, he was at the age where he would have to make his own way in the world. The friends of his who, like him, couldn't afford to attend a university were headed to the bigger cities, vying to get up with a big business and make a name for themselves, even if they faced a stiff headwind in not having the education those same businesses might be looking for. One or two were going to work on their family farms, the fate he so desperately had wanted to avoid. Eventually they would assume total responsibility for the farm. And then what? They would hope to have children. They would raise those children with the idea that they would one day inherit the farm. And on and on it went. Sam wasn't against it; he just knew it wasn't for him.

Other friends wanted to see the world, they would find work on merchant or fishing ships and then, if the pull of those jobs hadn't locked them into one already, they would pursue a career post-world journey. There were pragmatists among this loose circle of friends who had positioned themselves to formally continue their education, where they would step into the well-entrenched paths of doctors and lawyers.

It was a strange and novel thing, to be at that place where one said goodbye to the carefree pursuits of youth and looked at the trappings of adulthood before you.

To set aside the things one enjoyed in the name of real, honest work. Work that would, at best, be worthwhile and meaningful. And at worst, might be a task that at least provided a means to a living.

Why a lighthouse keeper? It seemed like a fine idea. He'd never been to the coast. Never seen a lighthouse. Only the stories he heard from Sean, who was passing along what he got from his brother's letters and infrequent trips back home. The letters told of mystery, allure and, he had accurately predicted, no chickens. The power. The responsibility; to be a beacon for people in their time of distress. To be significant. As quickly as these positive feelings rose within him, they were met by feelings of apprehension.

Was Armand a widower? Were all lighthouse keepers bachelors? True, Sean's brother wasn't, but was he the exception? Sam didn't want that. He wanted a family. He could envision children playing around the catwalk while he worked, him cautioning them to be careful and always hold onto the rail, his wife assisting him in the duties of maintaining the lighthouse. Family.

He tried reading more of the Jules Verne book; reading at night was usually a reliable recipe for bringing about sleep. Twenty minutes later, he was still reading, and sleep had crept no closer. He reached for the game, then his journal, but decided against both. He'd broken a record that day, and that was that. He dismissed the idea of drawing; it required a kind of focus that he didn't want to call on, not when he was trying to sleep and arguably lose focus. Why was it proving so hard to find sleep?

It was the lighthouse. The lighthouse and its noises. Beyond the mechanical noises of the lamp turning, the storm howled in the night, lashing the lighthouse with stinging rain and angry whitewater. The winds screamed like a banshee's wail, finding the crevices in the lighthouse to create the most awful, chilling moans. The banshee took turns at his windows, his eyes darted from one to the other with each flesh-crawling lament. Perhaps there were two banshees, his fear suggested, talking with one another in deciding his fate.

He tried to focus on something. The generator hum had been soothing at first but as the storm intensified, it had taken to intermittently groaning. What if it failed? Was there a back-up, or would they resort to candles and lanterns? His mind feverishly raced over countless possibilities. It dawned on him that he didn't know his way around the lighthouse. With the summer heat having exhausted itself at the end of August, Fall promised more frightful storms. Where were the blankets to keep them warm? What was in the crawlspace in his room?

It was the lighthouse. And it was the *lighthouse*. Once his father had secured a spot for him at Black Eagle, Sam had scoured the town, collecting all the books he could find on lighthouses. In it, there were drawings of lighthouses that connected to homes, positioned on cliffs well above the surf. There were other lighthouses shown, like Black Eagle, as standing alone. Some were isolated but on the mainland, and then there were others like this, on an island. This had led him to assume that, while their innerworkings might be different, while there might be room for more occupants in this lighthouse compared to that, the idea of a lighthouse was the same. But on that point, he was sorely mistaken.

Black Eagle Lighthouse was built on solid ground— stern, defiant black rock that had withstood nature's rage for generations. But beyond its rocky foundation, there was only sea. The deep, ill-tempered and insatiable wrath of the sea.

It was an isolation that caught him completely off guard. The isolation danced in the air, disrupting the stillness inside his room with every gust of wind, crawling across his flesh with ten thousand tiny probing insect legs. As he lay in the small, wooden frame of his bed, he could feel the ocean heave, as if it were rhythmically testing the strength and integrity of the lighthouse, and whether it might be uprooted.

There was nowhere to run. No escape. At one point, well after midnight he imagined, the storm's monstrous anger was throwing itself fully against the outer walls. The windows shook in their frames. The wind pushed water in between the bottom rail and the window sill, where it made a bubbling sound, as if boiling. The noise it made was like the gurgling of some mad, rabid creature. Sam sought comfort in rationalizing, but there was no comfort to be had, and his attempts at rational thought proved short-lived. Would a boat come for them? Not likely, not in this storm. He got out of bed at one point and peered out into the darkness.

The waves blossomed in devastating arcs that peaked more than halfway up the lighthouse. The captain who had delivered him earlier in the day was sharp and careful. A crew could perish in a storm like this, she wouldn't risk it. Maybe for Armand, but him? That only led his sinking down into the nauseating and delirious realization; they wouldn't tempt the tiny rowboat that bobbed helplessly underneath the dock. To do so would be inviting disaster, caught in the monster sea before they rounded the leeward side of the island. It would be like a mouse tempting a whale.

What if the sea won the battle this time, and took the lighthouse down? What if tonight was the night? Yes, it had stood for years against the strongest rage the sea could muster. But what if this storm was *the* storm to change that? Would Black Eagle collapse into itself, killing he and the lighthouse keeper instantly? That seemed coolly merciful. Or would the storm wound the lighthouse first, tearing some terrible gash into its side. Perhaps a well-placed bolt of lightning. The lighthouse would bleat like an injured sheep, seeking comfort that would not be delivered, except in devastation and death. He imagined the contents of his small, oddly-shaped room: the narrow three-drawered dresser, the little round table and accompanying stool, his bed—bleeding out of the hole in the wall, consumed by the voracious sea. Word would spread across the lands of the murderous storm that felled Black Eagle. Armand, known widely across the region, would be mourned, remembered for his decades of faithful service, for the lives he had no doubt saved through his dedication and vigilance on the watch. He, the lighthouse keeper's apprentice for less than a day, would be a footnote. An afterthought. He would never fall in love. Never have that family; never be given the chance to make a name for himself. At best, those he left behind would eulogize him, painting him in the loftiest of tones of who they believed he aspired to be.

It was maddening, and he couldn't shake loose from the feeling of his heart being in his throat. The night was a feverish rabbit hole that was filling fast with water.

There was something else that rattled his nerves about the way the wind shook the windows. Something that tugged urgently at consciousness even as he desperately sought sleep. It was the isolation of the lighthouse, the claustrophobia of his shuddering room, struggling to make sense of and find balance with the yawning expanse of the beckoning sea. On one hand, the terrible, choking confinement and separation of his new residence. Sounds that echoed vacantly off walls that seemed forever damp and forlorn. Places within those same walls that never saw the light of day. The lighthouse's interior aged in a way that felt ancient and forbidden, an obelisk that doubled as a mausoleum, stealing life one day at a time. And while he shared the residence with Armand, the old man could go a day without uttering a word. The lack of human interaction, the absence of other people...their voices, their smells...created a nauseating vertigo.

On the other hand, the immense vastness of water in every direction. The visceral, overwhelming invitation to bond with an elemental force, frightening and alluring with each enchanting wave. It was a freedom, daring to be embraced, if only he could look outside his constraining fears.

An hour before dawn, the banshees that had so successfully tormented his attempts at rest fled out to sea and left him to sleep.

When Sam woke, the storm was a distant cloud of dark, flickering etchings in the eastern sky. The sun broke through the tail-end of retreating storm clouds, promising to share its brilliance the rest of the day.

He felt rested, better than he thought he would, given how he tossed and turned throughout the night. The night's terrors felt removed and other-worldly, and he suppressed a feeling of embarrassment for the white-knuckle view he'd prescribed to the storm's passing. Outside, gulls squawked, no doubt scavenging among the cragged rocks for their morning's meal. At his little table, the dinner plate and cup of water had been replaced with a bowl of oatmeal decorated with slices of bananas and strawberries. Next to the bowl, an apple, newly arrived at the lighthouse from the previous evening's shipment. He was hungry, but there were more important matters requiring immediate attention.

He opened the door to his room. Even with the limited number of windows within, the inside of lighthouse was noticeably brighter in the light of day. The spiral staircase wrapped in either direction around a stone column, which served as the spine of the lighthouse. On each floor, a narrow walkway gave passage around the lighthouse's interior, providing access to the one or two rooms there. His room was on the sixth floor; he'd drawn a sketch of the lighthouse before ever setting foot on the island, and carried it with him in his knapsack. Sean had shared with him a detailed illustration of Black Eagle his brother had sent; Sam copied it line for line. While he hadn't been given a tour when he arrived last evening, he had a sense of the layout of the place.

The first floor was really nothing more than the entrance and storage, ironic and inefficient in that it was the largest floor of the nine. Armand kept a stack of wood opposite the entrance and furthest from any rain or weather that might find its way inside; the crew of the Viaje had unloaded more wood, along with fresh water, both of which were stored on the ground floor.

Near the entrance was stored the house trash. Some crates had been there when Sam arrived, leftovers from the previous supply run. In their hasty retreat from the storm, the crew had ferried them back onto the boat. There were two fishing poles and a net, and on the right side of the doorway, knobs lined the wall, each holding a coat of one sort or another. Next to that stood a small bureau. The only thing resting on its top was a pair of work gloves.

Up the stairs on the way to his bedroom, the oil room was on the second floor. Sam was unsure what the room might be used for today, since the lighthouse no longer operated on wicks and fuel. The third floor was also labeled as an oil room on his sketch, and the smell of oil had been oppressive here as they climbed the spiral. There was a strong humming coming from that room; the generator. In his sketch, the fourth floor was the store room, and the supplies scattered around its landing seemed to support that.

If his sketch were accurate, there would be a crane outside a large window on the fifth floor. This floor would also house a store room. Sam guessed the crane would be used for larger equipment, perhaps replacement parts if something mechanical broke down and couldn't be repaired.

Last night, he had gone no higher than his bedroom. There was another door opposite his. He went and checked it now; it was only a cleaning closet, with a mop, bucket, and handful of rags. It smelled of some menthol smell that was not unpleasant but, in the moment, irritated him. Above him on the seventh was the low light room, a room kept dark on purpose in order to look out for ships that might be in trouble. It was a novelty Sam had never considered; turning off the light to see better, but it made sense and he liked the idea.

The eighth floor would be Armand's bedroom, and nearest the service room on the 9th, with the catwalk and lantern above that.

He closed the closet door and turned his gaze up the staircase. Surely, Armand's room, at the very least his floor, would have what he was after. He bounded up the staircase, not bothering to stop on the low light floor. By the time he reached the eighth floor, he was a little winded. There were doors on either side of him, east and west if he had his bearings right. If that were so, the eastern door would be above his room, which told him that this door would lead to Armand's room. He stepped closer, but heard nothing within. The western door might be another closet, but it didn't seem likely. It had to be what he was looking for. He crossed the floor and swung open the door.

It was a bathroom in the purest sense of the word; a bladder of some kind, held up by a thoughtful arrangement of rope from the ceiling, hung over a large tub twice as big as the bladder itself. Aside from a small basin and a cup next to it with Armand's toothbrush, the room contained a handful of towels and a drying rack. Nothing that he needed.

Above him, he heard banging noises. Without closing the bathroom door, he dashed up the staircase. The noises were coming from the catwalk, and he didn't bother looking to see if Armand was in the service room.

The wind offered a soft, uneven howl as it blew across the mouth of the stairwell. Sam reached the catwalk and stopped.

He was spellbound by the view. The ocean writhed and coiled like some enormous blue serpent that seemed to surface wherever his gaze went. In the distance, the ocean and sky blended in a grey haze; a fog followed in trace of the bad weather from the night before. Sam drew his gaze in closer and saw silent flashes, some unspoken, preternatural language as waves crested, fretting foamy white caps before subsiding. Then another wave followed a short distance from the first. And another there. It reminded him of a story Sean had relayed to him. Sean's family had traveled to the coast to visit his brother. He recounted how they went out on the water one day, and their ship was overtaken by a pod of dolphins. They made no noise. A shiny, glistening fin would rise gracefully out of the water before disappearing back into the sea, followed by another some distance away, and on and on. There was no rhythm Sam could discern amongst the waves, yet he had the inescapable feeling there was one. It wasn't orchestrated, yet it was nature's glorious symphony.

The wind was adamant, pressing at his back, while hurriedly pushing the remnants of the night's storm out of sight. A large, rusty pole clanged against the catwalk railing; the pole was bent slightly, as if it had held something, perhaps a flag or banner of some kind, and the force of the wind had ripped it from against the upper rail. It was the pole that occupied his host's attention at the moment.

Armand was dressed in a tan longshoreman's coat, and a black watch-cap held down the thinning grey hair that fluttered in the breeze as if trying to escape. A necklace hung around his neck. Sam had seen it the night before, but couldn't make out the thing at the end of the necklace. Today, he saw it was a small compass.

"Good morning, I need—"

"What?" Armand replied, still focused on the pole.

Sam raised his voice. "I'm looking for a toilet."

Armand withdrew a hammer from his coat and began banging on the pole in an attempt to straighten it. As he hammered, the bottom section of the pole jarred loose from its remaining fastening. The vibration surprised Armand, and he lost his grip. The pole fell, skittering down the side of the lighthouse in a clumsy plummet before striking the ground and cartwheeling excitedly with a loud clang! into the rocks on the water's edge. Armand peered down, let out a hearty laugh and turned, wide-eyed, to Sam. "Indeed you are."

A bucket. That was the toilet. The bucket, or the hole in the ground where the bucket's contents would be deposited. There had once been an outhouse on the leeward side, Armand shared, but a rogue wave had come in at an odd angle from the south and swept it away. The hole the outhouse covered still served its purpose; from time to time, Armand would pour some lime into the hole. The idea that Sam would have a chamber pot in his bedroom was a letdown. It was primitive. Black Eagle had electricity!

"Yes, that is true." Armand replied as he walked with Sam down the stairs and back to his bedroom. "Electricity and plumbing are not the same thing."

And with that, Armand opened Sam's bedroom door, handed him a roll of toilet paper and went down the stairs.

"The bucket on the right," Armand said over his shoulder, "Use that one. The other one is for washing and such. Don't get them confused."

Once he had answered nature's call, Sam got his tour of his new home.

There was no running water, nor would there be for the foreseeable future. The wash basins and bathtub drained out of the side of the lighthouse by means of small outlet pipes. Water could be heated, if desired, over an open fire for bathing.

The layout of Black Eagle was fairly accurate in comparison to the sketch he'd made. In his sketch, the second floor had been an oil storage room. Now, Armand had converted it into the most breathtaking and unusual garden. A single pillar stood in the center of the room, adorned with mirrors from the floor to the ceiling. The pillar bisected the two windows on either side of the outer wall. In each window, mirrors had been placed at certain angles. Along the walls of the room, placed at irregular intervals, were plants of all types. A pot here, a rectangular garden box there. The mirrors in the windows sent sunlight to the mirrors affixed to the pillar. These mirrors were at different angles which, as the sun rose in the morning sky, carried the sun's rays onto the various plants in the room. Sam guessed the whole setup meant some of these plants got four to six hours of morning sun. He smelled basil, parsley, and the strong aroma of mint.

The fourth floor was a model of efficiency; shelves lined the side walls, with canned goods neatly organized by size and type. An elevated floor underneath the lowest shelf held dried goods like flour, sugar, and oats. Along the outer wall, another basin and another bladder, these for cooking. On the right side of the basin, a small drying rack propped up dishes from the prior evening, a towel crisply folded over top of them. To its left, there was a small stove, still putting out heat from the morning's meal. The room smelled of burnt wood, citrus, and eggs.

He had been partially correct about the fifth floor; there was a crane. More than that, there was a door that led to a small platform, upon which the crane's cargo could be delivered. The platform was ten feet across and extended out five feet from the lighthouse. On either side of the door were positioned two rain barrels; the water that was used in the kitchen and for bathing.

They skipped the lowlight room; Sam felt confident he knew what was inside and Armand offered nothing to suggest otherwise.

The day was stretching into the early afternoon as they completed the tour, and Sam stayed glued to Armand's hip as the older man went about his regular tasks.

They started at the top of Black Eagle, cleaning the windows of the lantern. The pole that had fallen would have to be retrieved and put back in place. It was used to signal ships, with an assortment of flags Armand kept in the floor below. But the replacing of the fixture would be a task for another day.

After the windows, Armand cleaned the lantern lens. That was followed by a thorough assessment of all lighthouse windows and sills to determine if the night's storm had damaged something that would need replacing. Despite what Sam concluded was a ferocious storm, the windows and their frames were all intact. Armand swept the stairs, frequently looking out the windows for any ships in distress, but finding none. There was a routine maintenance and health check on the generator, to include checking its fuel levels. Every two hours, Armand logged the weather.

The days progressed, with Armand gradually turning over more and more tasks to Sam. It was invigorating work, and purposeful. It was work that Sam picked up easily and enthusiastically, every chore contributing in some small way or another to keeping the lighthouse running and providing its beacon to those at sea. Armand spoke more frequently, offering insights as to the order he preferred to do the day's tasks, sharing a story about a ship he'd helped rescue, or recounting when a gam of whales took up residence near the lighthouse for the better part of a week.

Sam grew to like Armand, and respected the pace and determination at which the older man kept the lighthouse running. He thought how frenzied it must have been when lighthouses burned traditional wicks with oil, and how the keepers took shifts to man the house throughout the night. Now, an alarm would sound if the light went out for any reason. If the main light failed, there was a small Fresnel lens and three days' worth of fuel dedicated to it. The Fresnel wasn't as powerful as the main lantern, but would suffice until repairs could get it up and running once again.

Sam passed his down time thinking of home and what his father might be doing. He fought to keep his thoughts from going to his mother, but it was a pathway he'd well excavated in his mind, and he didn't yet comprehend the troughs he had created in his thinking. The solitude of the lighthouse gave him more time to think which, in turn, only deepened some of his thought patterns. When the reflections of his mother proved to be overwhelming and carried him near the shores of despair, he would find solace in the garden room. There, the smells reminded him of the garden she kept outside the south wall of their house. There he found peace and, in his mind, believed himself closer to wherever she might now be.

On other occasions, he dreamt of what it might be like to be the keeper of his own lighthouse. If Black Eagle had taught him anything, it was that he wanted to run a lighthouse on the mainland, with a house attached to it, or at the very least within walking distance. He would hope he would find a wife that was keen on running the lighthouse too. She would be smart and independent, smarter than he in that she was less impulsive, more practical. More focused. They would complement one another perfectly. He could hear the laughter as their children played in the yard, the wild, carefree giggles of youth. A boy and a girl. Twins, he allowed the thought with delight. They would grow up healthy and loved, and if they couldn't afford to attend the university, would have the chance to run the lighthouse, just like their father. When they took over, he might go back to writing. Then one day, he would buy a large private ship and sail his wife around the world.

It was a dream, a vision, that his father would find pleasing.

He was lost in thoughts like these one evening, standing outside the ground floor of the lighthouse. The winds were a warm, calm kind of constant, carrying the most pleasant smell of saltwater, and the waves lapped casually against the rocks. The moon was rising in a clear sky as Armand came down.

Sam smiled to his mentor and went back to looking out at the sea. Armand didn't move. After a few moments, Sam turned back to look at him. Armand continued to stare at his apprentice, sizing him up.

"Tomorrow," the older man said, "Your learning begins."

CHAPTER THREE

ILL WITH DISTRACTION

The next day started no differently than had the previous fourteen, not that Sam could tell. But he felt off. He was nervous, apprehensive even as they started the day's tasks. He had slept fitfully the night prior, wrestling with the cryptic message Armand had left him with. They got to the lens room and Sam discovered just how different the day would be. A series of scratches covered one of the lenses.

At first glance, Sam thought Armand was playing some kind of joke on him, but one look at his mentor told him there was no trick to be had. Armand's face was grave.

"A bird. Perhaps a gull. This has happened once before."

Armand went on to explain how on one previous occasion a large Wandering albatross had made its way into the lantern room. The bird could not figure out how to get out, and when Armand found it, the floor of the lantern room was littered with little feathers and bird shit. In agitation, the bird had clawed at the lens, scratching it enough it required replacing.

Armand surveyed the lens and surrounding area. Feathers danced along the floor with the slightest disturbance in the air. His face perched on a ledge of indifference before falling into a frown. "We'll need to swap this one out."

"The scratches don't look that bad to me," Sam countered. It was true; yes they were visible, but certainly they wouldn't prevent the light from coming through.

"Think of the lens as an eye," Armand said, as he continued sizing up the lens, "a scratch on the eye makes it harder to see, no matter how small the scratch itself may be. The same is true here. An untarnished lens can shine for over thirty kilometers."

"These scratches will reduce that distance?"

"By as much as half."

Sam understood Armand's concern. Though the scratches were only on one lens face, the reduction in range could be treacherous if the sea conditions were bad. "Will it be difficult to replace?"

Armand's frown softened. "Easier than replacing an eye."

The good news was the replacement lens was close by; in the small cubby inside Sam's room. Less thrilling was its weight. To replace the twenty-one-inch-tall lens would be a two-man lift, as it weighed almost as much as the two of them combined.

The hardest part of the whole task was getting the lens from its slot inside the cubby and carrying to the top of the lighthouse. Sam stumbled a few times and nearly lost his grip, but managed until they reached the catwalk.

The whole replacing process took no more than 30 minutes; Sam didn't think it was much of a setback in terms of completing the day's tasks. During the repair, Sam kept himself busy with his ball-and-cup game. One thing he had come to appreciate about life in a lighthouse— there was plenty of time to get good at things, and he had invested a hefty amount of free time to improve his skills at this game. He had the lofty aspiration of getting to five hundred catches, and knew that with practice and patience, it was only a matter of time.

The window repair complete, Armand ask Sam to sweep the stairs while he finished installing the lens.

It was Sam's least favorite chore, monotonous and long. Nine floors' of stairs everyday seemed excessive. And for what? There was never really anything on them beyond dust and the odd scrap of paper or food. He began sweeping.

To keep his mind busy, he thought of home. His mind replied with a memory of having to sweep after dinner, one of his regular chores. This thought only served to make him frustrated. Like here, it didn't matter how well he had swept the previous day, there was always more dirt and dust to be collected there too. The world was full of dirt and dust, with the occasional pile of chicken crap. He actually felt himself getting angry, and went to the thing that brought him the most joy; his game.

There were really three elements to the game. Of course, there was the ball, the string, and the stick with the tiny cup. But, in playing the game there were three things to consider: the toss, the pop, and the catch.

The toss was simple. They key with the toss was not to propel the ball up with too much force, whether you were just starting a fresh round and the ball was free floating, or it was in the cup and you were launching it for another catch. If you went too strong, the string would go taut, which would jerk the ball down and increase the chance of missing it. Too weak, and you didn't give yourself any space to catch it.

The "pop" was what the apprentice called the movement of the ball immediately after the toss. A straight "up and down" pop resulting from a perfect toss was ideal in that you had to do the least amount of maneuvering of the cup.

He dissected and analyzed his playing of the game as he swept. So caught up in his thoughts, he failed to notice Armand waiting for him at the first-floor landing as he finished. He wiped the forehead from his brow and started back up the stairs.

"What are you doing?" Armand asked, his voice a growl.

It was a tone Sam hadn't heard previously from his host. He had been doing the same thing he'd done for the last few weeks; sweeping from the outside of the step in, so that the debris being swept might fall down on the stairs underneath or, with luck, all the way down to the ground floor. He thought back to his actions and realized he'd neglected to sweep the contents on the ground floor. He descended the stairs and moved to the middle of the room.

"No. Stop." The tone hadn't left Armand's voice. If anything, it had settled in. "Do you know how long it took you to finish the stairs?"

Sam had no idea. It was a long time. He shrugged.

"Forty-three minutes." Armand replied, swinging his pocket watch from its chain.

"That seems right. There are a lot of steps."

"A lot of steps." Armand parroted. He walked to Sam and took the broom from him. He calmly walked to the bottom of the stairs and held the broom out in front of him. "Sweep them again."

"What? I just finished."

"Quite right." Armand said.

He walked back to the center of the room where Sam stood and swept the debris there into a small pile.

When he was finished, he tossed the broom in Sam's direction. Sam caught it, a look of surprise washing over his face. Armand scooped up the pile with his hands and proceeded towards the stairs. He started walking up the stairs, ever so gently shaking his hands. The debris sifted through the cracks between his fingers and over the edge of his palms, misting down onto the stairs in barely visible hazy wanderings.

"What are you doing?" Sam asked.

"Providing incentive." Armand replied dryly. Up the stairs he went. Sam followed.

They reached the top of the lighthouse. Armand reached out his hand for the broom, and Sam handed it to him. Armand briskly swept the top step with a few strong sweeps before moving to the next one. He moved across it, outside to in, with three strong sweeps. He turned and pushed the broom into Sam's chest.

"That...is sweeping."

Sam's confusion gave way to frustration that further eroded the anger he felt welling up inside him. "Silly old man. What you are talking about? That's exactly the same thing I was doing."

Unfazed, Armand began heading down the stairs. "Fine, then do it again."

With a surge of emotion, Sam swept. He looked over his shoulder at Armand as the older man descended the stairs. What kind of incentive was this? It was madness, is what it was. Had Armand actually just dropped dirt on the stairs again? The crazy fool. Sam would show him.

He made it down to his bedroom floor and noticed his door was open. There was a cup of water on the table. He took it and downed it in three hearty gulps. He sat down in the chair and realized he was breathing heavy. He didn't want to have to do the stairs again, so quickly got up and got back to work.

Armand was organizing the crates for the trash when Sam finished the stairs a second time. Sam looked at him, confident that he had done a crisp, efficient job.

Armand placed a crate on top of another. "Do you know how many stairs there are from top to bottom?"

"Stairs? No." It wasn't something Sam had ever thought about. "Eighty?"

"One hundred and forty-four. Do you know how long it took you to clean them this last time?"

Sam shook his head.

"Twenty-six minutes."

Sam took in a deep breath as his chest swelled. "I almost cut my time in half."

Armand adjusted his glasses at the end of his nose and frowned without looking up from his watch. "Yes. True. And yet it you were truly focused it would take you even less time."

Sam looked at Armand, then walked to the room center and looked up. It was a dizzying view. He couldn't believe there were less than one hundred fifty stairs;

it felt like twice that many. And how much more time could he cut out of the whole affair?

"If you're focused, you should be able to clean the stairs completely in less than ten minutes."

"That's ludicrous." Sam said, a laugh escaping before he could stop it.

Armand grabbed the broom and went to the bottom step. He swept from the outside in with five successive sweeps, counting aloud as he did.

"One, two, three, four."

"Each step takes four seconds. If you want to do the math, you're welcome to."

Armand held the broom out at arm's length and let go. The broom balanced on its bristles before falling towards Sam, who caught it as Armand ascended the stairs.

They broke for lunch. Sam's frustration lingered, and he was unable to shake it. Ten minutes to sweep nine flights of stairs seemed outlandish. His mind grappled with the possibility of ulterior motives. Was it some rite of passage that new apprentices underwent? Perhaps this was what passed for entertainment for the old man. He thought to ask Armand about the matter, but his anger had turned to resentment and he went straight to his room from downstairs.

He was too upset to play his game and tried to read, but found himself staring out in the window at the vast ocean. There was nothing different about his sweeping today than in days past. Why now? He tried to swallow the displeasure, but replaying it in his mind only served to regurgitate it over and over again.

"Lunch."

No knock on the door, no opening the door to invite him down to the kitchen to grab his food.

He wouldn't eat. That would show Armand. He knew what he was doing around this place. The stairs would always need sweeping. Weather would constantly need to be recorded. He would skip lunch and show the old man that even hungry, he could perform all the duties required of a keeper.

It was a foolish plan. The thought rolled over him like a strong wave. He would be hungry. Hunger would lead to irritability, and he was already in something of a knot. Maybe he would ask for an apology. An explanation as to why this expectation of fast sweeping hadn't been explained earlier. Yes, that seemed appropriate. If he needed to be stern with the old man, he would be. He could demand an answer if it came right down to it. Was Armand going to say no? Sam laughed.

Armand liked to eat lunch sitting on the catwalk, looking at the ocean. Sam's plate would be waiting for him in the kitchen. He would grab it and join Armand up top, and see how things unfolded from there. He opened his bedroom door to leave.

Armand stood there, holding both plates. "You have a very common disease."

He thrust a plate into Sam's chest. Sam took the plate and followed Armand up the stairs.

"Disease? What are you talking about? I'm as healthy as a porpoise."

Armand kept walking. "Diseased."

The old man must be losing hold of his senses. That seemed plausible. First, the sweeping situation, now this.

There were other signs that suggested madness was encroaching on his host like a high tide; gradual but unmistakable. There was the garden. Yes, it was incredible, but it also seemed a little crazy. On several occasions over the past few weeks, Sam heard the old man talking. Initially, he thought someone had arrived at Black Eagle. But it was the plants. Armand was talking to the plants. And not in some silly way, like a grandfather might talk to his grandchildren, or a child talking to a puppy. He was having conversations. Talking about the weather. His breakfast. Nonsense.

If it wasn't the plants, he was talking to himself. Ludicrous and bizarre, self-evident things. "This is the thirteenth step" or "there are three gulls on that rock". And it wasn't like Sam was standing next to him, or walking with him when Armand uttered these things. No. Sam could be on the far side of the catwalk, or in another room. If the old man thought his apprentice was closer when he was speaking, he gave no hint of it.

Then there was the morning ritual Armand had of sitting cross-legged on the ground floor on a small mat. Just sitting. Eyes closed. Sam happened on this by chance one morning when he awoke early needing to relieve himself. He brought the bucket downstairs and there was Armand, still in his robe, sitting on the floor. Sam thought him a fool. These odd events together were cause enough to re-think this entire venture. Sam had no desire to take over Black Eagle; it was too far from anywhere, and there wasn't room to raise a family besides. Someone from the mainland would have to be told. Someone would have to step into this role. Armand would go away to the places where they put people who weren't right in their head. But his actions seemed proof-positive that this kind of solitude really did drive a person crazy.

"I'm not mad." Armand said as they passed the seventh floor.

It was Sam's turn to stop. Had he been talking out loud?

They ate in silence—Armand at his usual pace, Sam anxiously swallowing his meal. When he finished, he broke the swollen silence between them.

"What disease are you talking about?"

Armand set his plate down next to him. He ran his

fingers through his beard, inspected what morsels had been caught there, and rubbed his hands together. "The disease of distraction."

Sam started to protest, but Armand cut him off.

"Your thinking is distracted. Distracted thinking makes it harder to accomplish things. Look at that ship."

He pointed to the north. Several miles away from them, a large schooner headed west, its sails gleaming in the sun and full of a steady wind. Armand continued.

"Focus on that ship. By focus, I mean direct your attention to it."

Sam looked at the ship. "Okay."

Now, assign it some meaning." Armand grew animated. He stood, walking to the railing nearest the ship.

"What do you mean?"

"Imagine for example, it's a ship in distress. That 'meaning' leads to possible actions, right? We might light the lamp, signal the coastal guard or, were they closer, row out to see how we might assist."

Sam set his plate down and joined Armand on the railing. "I guess so."

"Of course," Armand continued. "Now, don't focus on the ship."

"What?"

"Ignore the ship for a moment. Ignore it, and all the meaning we just assigned to it."

"Okay."

Nearby, there were a flight of three seagulls riding the afternoon breeze. Sam looked at them. He smiled. They were so free. He noticed how they hardly flapped their wings; just rode the currents provided them.

"Very good." Armand said. "Now direct your attention back to the ship."

Sam did so.

"Now, imagine that ship has pirates on it."

Sam smiled. He thought of Kongre, the pirate leader from the book he'd brought with him. The ship was headed this way, he imagined, seeking treasure buried somewhere with the inhospitable rock of Black Eagle.

"Focus. Meaning. Action." Armand said matter-of-factly. "This is our first crucial decision cycle. If those are pirates, our actions would be very different than if it were a ship in distress. A person's life...how they view their past, how they live in the present, and how they look to the future...all depend on the meaning they assign to each."

"Focus...meaning...action." Sam repeated.

Armand turned to look at his apprentice. "So, when you were sweeping earlier, were you thinking about sweeping?"

Sam sheepishly shook his head. He had been thinking about anything but sweeping. Lunch, home, his game. He hadn't been focused on what was right in front of him in the slightest.

The three gulls swooped overhead and dove toward the island. The two men watched the birds fluster and land on rocks a few feet above the waterline.

"Can you focus on the birds and the ship at the same time?"

Sam thought about this for a moment. "Well..."

"You can visualize the birds with a ship," Armand finished his thought for him. "But you cannot focus on the birds below and the ship in the distance at the same time."

Sam was silent, but he understood what Armand was saying.

"Now," Armand said, "to bring the point home, imagine that ship is bringing your parents..."

Sam grabbed the older man by the arm. Armand saw a pained expression flower across his apprentice's face.

"No."

Unfazed, Armand went immediately in another direction.

"The second decision we need to look at is, what kind of questions do we ask ourselves?"

Sam released his hold on the emotions that were welling up inside him.

"I don't understand what you mean."

Armand picked up a small piece of bread from his plate. With a mischievous grin, he threw it off the catwalk in the direction of the three gulls, his eyes following it down. The bread fell in a wavy, windy line and landed atop an outcropping of rock. One of the gulls spied it first, followed by the other two. The first gull led a concert of shrieks as it flew to the outcropping, pecked at the bread and missed. The morsel popped into the air, leading to a jousting frenzy before the first gull triumphantly nabbed the morsel and flew to another rock.

Armand grinned in delight. "The questions we ask ourselves are the pathway to the kind of life we will have."

"Explain more," Sam said, intrigued.

Armand scratched his beard, reminding Sam of a dog feverishly scratching at fleas. Such an odd man.

"If I wake every morning with the thought, 'what dread is life going to throw my way today', my mind will come up with an answer. 'Mind' will respond with something like, 'today you're going to have a terrible argument with your brother' or 'today you're going to step in a puddle and ruin your shoes'. In other words, 'mind' will look for things to make my day full of dread."

"That's silly. No one asks themselves that question."

"Possibly true," Armand said, finally leaving his beard alone, "but people talk negatively to themselves moreso than the opposite. More than that, they worry about the things beyond their control."

"Tell me more." Sam looked at Armand, a kind of admiration filling out his face.

"Think of the pirates," Armand said, motioning with his head in the direction of the ship, "you can't control whether they come here or not. If you worry about it, what do you accomplish?"

Sam shrugged.

"Quite right. In fact, worrying about their invasion takes away from the time you have to prepare for their invasion. Preparation is within your control. What the pirates do is not."

Journal Entry: Today was an interesting day. I'm exhausted and still not convinced Armand isn't crazy. I had to fight back tears when he suggested my parents were on a ship far from us. It makes me think of you, mother. I hope I am making you proud.

Crazy or not, long after we finished the day's tasks, his words stayed with me, and if I'm honest with myself, I wanted to hear more. We picked up on our catwalk conversation at dinner. He expanded on some of the things we had discussed earlier. I'm not sure it all makes sense, but I surprised myself by grabbing for my journal, even before readying for bed, to write down all the recollections from the day.

1. **What we focus on**—*this is the most important decision we can make. We can put our energy towards things we can control, or lose it by focusing on the things we can't control. We can direct our focus to the past, the present, or the future.*

2. What meaning do we assign to it—*the meaning we give to the thing we focus on creates the feelings. Two people can look at the same thing and have completely different feelings. This is based on their experiences, their thought patterns, and their values and beliefs. The past, present, and future all have different meanings, depending on the meaning we assign to them. (Must ask Armand more about this...isn't my past unchangeable?) The feelings that come from the meaning given lead to...*

3. What actions we take—*based on the meaning we attach to what we focus on, we choose what to do. We develop patterns of thoughts. These patterns become habits. These habits become our beliefs. These beliefs become our lives.*

We cannot focus on two things at once...Armand said this. It seems so obvious, and yet I play with the idea over and over in my mind. He said, 'there can only be one master' and I'm quite certain I don't know what he's talking about.

Further, he said the quality of the questions we ask ourselves leads us to the quality of our lives. If we ask questions about why life is unfair, our mind will come up with answers to reinforce that perspective. But if we ask what are the things that make life so enjoyable, the mind will answer that question in a similar fashion. If I understood him correctly, we are 'focusing' our lives by the types of questions we ask ourselves. Focus on what is good, and we foster and attract more goodness into our lives. Focus on what is bad, and we attract more misfortune.

The sky is filling with clouds. Funny how I never would have paid much attention to something like that when I was back home. Now, I pay attention to the clouds, the wind, the color of the sky in the morning and at night. If I'm reading the clouds right, we'll see a storm tomorrow.

CHAPTER FOUR

TEMPEST: A CRY FOR HELP

A flurry of gulls had gathered overhead, screaming warnings to one another as they darted high, then low, anxiously vying for position over some morsel the turbulent waters had thrown up somewhere in the rocks on the windward side of Black Eagle island. The clouds seemed to scramble over one another as well, as the storm had been gathering all day continued to warn of its impending arrival. The sea was a roiled stain of blue-green with spitting white caps that marched fearlessly with the tempest.

The day felt frantic. Sam had slept well the night prior, but had woken late. This feeling of being behind in his chores carried with it a far more frightening feeling. He felt like he was hurtling towards something. It was beyond unpleasant. It was scary.

He wanted more answers from Armand, more time to dive further into their discussion from the previous day, but free time was proving difficult to find and, as the day progressed, the feeling of...collision, was that accurate?... grew stronger. More certain. *We'll talk tonight* was all he could muster from the old man as they passed by one another, which did nothing to release the buildup of pressure.

Sam stayed on the catwalk, the wind shrieking across the lantern house. There was flashes of lightning to the east, but the grumbles of thunder were still too far away to be heard. It was an undeniable truth that his mind often went to different places when he was doing his daily tasks, but it had always been that way. He assumed that was true for most people; they worked on things with their body while their mind did its own housekeeping.

In the light of day, Armand's alternative—sustained focus—seemed unrealistic. Life was full of too many variables. People needed time to process things. How could one control their mind? It was laughable.

The old man talked about each thought was a sacred thing, with every negative thought a seed that, if fed any attention, would grow into a weed in the mind. The same was true for positive thoughts; given the light of the mind's eye, they could blossom into the most beautiful flowers.

Then Armand had talked about purpose, and about how the events of one's life weren't random at all. That life was some grand play for each person, and that the things that happened to a person were intended to happen for them, even the suffering they faced. When the old man said this, Sam wondered if his father had shared with Armand what had happened to his mother. But why would he have? And what happened to his mother was not part of any grand design. It wasn't God, it wasn't fate. It was...

He let the thought trail off. His mind came back to what Armand had said about purpose. It was a questionable prospect, but an idea, a seed born somewhere deep within him, had sprouted in his mind. Writing. When he wrote, there was something that happened to him. Something that happened to his thinking. Things slowed down. There was his pencil, and the pad of paper, and whatever he was writing. Sometimes he wrote about things he saw in the world. On other occasions, he wrote whatever came to mind. During these moments, the world seemed to dissolve, *did* dissolve. Did he think during those moments? He wasn't sure he did...or at least, he wasn't *in his head*. That inner voice, that ever-present monologue, wasn't. And that was a very interesting feeling.

Was that what Armand was trying to suggest?

Dinner was later than normal, and the murmurs of thunder that preceded dinner had become cannon roars by the time they were finished rinsing the plates. The lantern was on, and the storm seemed to respond to its unfaltering eye as if it were a challenge. It lashed the catwalk with whipping winds and sideways rains.

Armand took dinner in his room. He didn't always, and tonight Sam felt like it was intentional. Perhaps he had offended his host. He had let slip a few comments that betrayed the thoughts he had about the old man's state of mind and, given time to reflect, now felt shame for having been so critical of a man who had taken him in and was teaching in his craft. He felt the twisting nag of an apology growling in his stomach.

For his part, Sam took dinner in the garden on the second floor. It had become something of a routine for him, and usually Armand joined him. Armand was very focused in his conversations and when he held them. Sam noticed that in the garden room, the old man only ever asked questions. He wanted to know about Sam's upbringing, but managed to avoid ever asking directly about his mother. A few nights before, Armand had asked him what he dreamed of doing and if he had always wanted to be a lighthouse keeper.

It was then that Sam admitted he liked to write. He had forgotten that 'writing' had been his answer when Armand had asked the question about what he really wanted to do. Forgotten the bulk of that conversation until right this very moment.

Writing wasn't something he normally shared with people, and certainly not as a means of making a living. It was something personal. The thought of someone reading and not liking his work wrenched his insides in a manner he didn't care for. Much easier to keep his writing to himself. Easier. Safer. He didn't think it was very good anyhow, he just liked it.

Armand had probed on the subject. What kind of things did he like to write? What compelled him to write? How did writing make him feel? Sam had answered each question, and thought the questions came from a place of boredom on behalf of his host.

The garden room made him feel alive. One minute, the smell of mint would dominate the air, the next, rosemary washed over his senses. Just sitting in the room made every meal better. He had arrived at a place where he appreciated the isolation and solitude the lighthouse afforded, parts of him even welcomed those sensations. At the same time, the chronic tang of wet stone occasionally intermingled with generator fuel drove him to spend time outside the lighthouse, or up on the catwalk when he wasn't working. This brought some relief, but when on the ground he quickly realized that he traded fuel and stone for the salty mix of ocean and wet rock, with the all-too-frequent rancid stench of dead fish. The garden brought air he labeled as 'fresh' and, later he would realize, brought fresh perspective into his life.

The winds howled their banshee's howl, a sound he had become accustomed to and not completely comfortable with. The storm was a barrage of lightning flashes and furious pelting sheets on the windows. With no company and the day's efforts now catching up with him, Sam decided he might skip his journal writing and go straight to sleep.

"Help!"

The cry rang off the interior lighthouse walls. Sam wasn't sure from where exactly the cry had originated, but leapt from his chair, nearly knocking over his plate and cup in the process. He whipped open the garden door and started taking the stairs in threes. There were many procedures he had been taught over the weeks on Black Eagle, but Armand getting injured had not been one of them.

The sound of Armand's bedroom door opening stopped Sam in his tracks.

"Sir, are you well?"

"Help!"

The cry again. It wasn't Armand at all. It was outside. Somewhere in the dark. In the storm. A sailor. Perhaps a ship had floundered, or someone had fallen overboard in the choppy waters. But why would a boat have tempted this storm?

Sam continued up the stairs, headed towards the lantern room, but Armand redirected him.

"The lowlight room!" the keeper barked.

Sam reached the landing on the seventh floor. A brilliant, bluish light flashed out from underneath the lowlight room door. It wasn't a bolt of lightning. There was no decay of brightness; the light rippled under the door in uneven shudders, like a thing alive. It cast the landing in an eerie and surreal glow. He felt the dread, the fear that had been gathering all day in his stomach move now into his throat.

Armand came down from his room and stood next to the door. The light coming from within the room seemed drawn to the old man; it grew brighter next to where he stood and went towards his heel the way a loyal dog might to its master. He beckoned Sam closer, then opened the door.

The glow was nearly blinding, and didn't appear to come from any single source within the room. The entire room was emanating this blue-white shimmering brilliance. It was warm. Something inside the room called to Sam. Collision flashed through his consciousness. Some unseen messenger, or some thing, beckoned from within. Sam blinked, the lotus of fear in his throat flowered, and he stepped into the room.

When he opened his eyes, the room was gone. He and Armand stood on the roof of some strange tower, underneath a brightly lit canopy of stars. The sky was odd. Different. No, not the sky, a voice in his head interjected, the light. The light was different. The storm was gone. It was night, but unlike any night he'd ever witnessed.

Though there was no moon, the night sky was illuminated as if the moon were at its fullest, and nearer to the earth than it had ever been. When Sam scanned the sky, looking for the source of the light, he found none. He only noticed that wherever he looked was brighter than the sky in his peripheral vision. Looking down, there was water in every direction, glittering like a million diamonds in the sparkling blue light of this strange night. The breeze was warm, tender even, so unlike the cold, harsh nights they'd recently been experiencing.

After a moment, Sam noticed that wherever he cast his gaze in the ocean, the area became brighter than the areas surrounding it, similar to the sky. Not only that, but he could see much further than he ever had before.

I must be dreaming, he thought to himself. And though he was quite certain he hadn't expressed the thought out loud, he heard it echo, like a distant bird's cry, in the air around them.

"What is this place?"

Armand stood next to him. "This is your mind."

Sam processed what he had just heard. "That isn't possible. What happened to the lighthouse?"

"It is still there. And we are there too. But we are also here."

"I don't understand. How?"

"How." The old man paused, chewing on the question. "Do you want to leave? You can. You can take two steps backward. You will be outside the entryway to the lowlight room. This will be as if a dream. When you awake in the morning, you will be able to continue your apprenticeship. You will close this door of belief and step through another one."

Sam looked to Armand, then looked back at the water. His fear was gone. There was only calm. Yes, calm. Something inside him, not the voice that normally occupied his head he noted, told him this was the collision. Something he feared had brought him peace. It was a transcendent thought, and one he so wanted to explore further, but Armand had lain a decision at his feet.

Sam shook his head no.

"Your mind," Armand continued. "is the ocean you see before you. Every incident of your life, every person you've ever met, resides somewhere in these waters."

Armand stepped forward, opening his arms to the vast expanse before them. Sam was unsteady, unsure. But he took a step forward as Armand explained further.

"Your memories are here. Your fears. Your hopes and your dreams. Your ambitions. Your rituals and routines, the trance-like rhythm of your life...they are all before you. Look around, in every direction. Look closely."

Sam did as Armand instructed. He turned in a complete circle. There was land, but it was dark and so far off as to be nearly imperceptible. Yet he knew it was there. There was no manmade light, no coastline with the beacon of some town that might serve as a point of reference. But there was water. Plenty of water. He noted that, when he cast his vision out to the horizon, some areas didn't light up as brightly as did others. In these spots, the waters seemed murky, shrouded in a dense fog. In other areas, as his vision adjusted to the immense distances, storm clouds flashed thick under shudders of lightning. In those areas, the water erupted in galloping waves that clashed against one another, and he felt a swell of apprehension when he looked into the storm. In still other spots, it was nearly sunny if such a thing was possible in this place, with calm, placid waters. He thought he saw schools of fish under these waters, and was sure that dolphins glided through the waves in majestic arcs.

He fixed his gaze upon this last spot and focused.

The waters grew brighter, and transformed into a memory. He was a toddler. Perhaps as old as two. He had just finished a bath and was triumphantly parading around naked, while his mother chased after him, towel in her hand. He understood, looking back into this memory, his younger self thought this a game; the more she chased, the faster he ran. They were both laughing, even as she called him by his name, imploring him to stand still. He ran from the bath, trotting into the kitchen and making a wild circle around their dinner table, a shrill squeal of unbridled joy erupting from his mouth. His mother closed in behind him.

The table seemed large, but Sam knew it was only because he was so small in this moment of his life. More laughter followed from behind only challenged him, spurring him on faster. He widened his counterclockwise arc around the table. Unbeknownst to his younger self, his mother changed direction and ran clockwise. He turned the corner at the head of the table and there she was, the bright smile of wonder and surprise on her face, towel opened and ready to snare him.

He stopped in his tracks, brought his hands to either side of his face without touching it, and squealed in delight. Sensing he'd been caught, or instinctively wanting his mother's loving embrace, he charged forward, shouting *"MOMM-EEE!"* as she enveloped him into the inviting confines of his towel.

Sam pulled back from the memory. The rapturous joy he'd felt moments before left him, like water dripping through his fingers.

He moved his view further in this part of the ocean, a part that seemed to welcome the sun under a blanket of stars. A dolphin bolted straight out of the water, flapped its tail forming itself into a crescent moon, and dove down headfirst into the waves. He followed it with his eyes.

Another memory. This time he was older. School age, but still young. He was playing hide and seek. There was the indignant caterwaul of a classmate protesting having been found, followed by the barking retort of the rules being fair and square, concluded finally by stuttering resignation.

He was hiding in a thick bush, one of several that lined the wall of the school. The air had a hint of coolness to it, and oak leaves were just beginning to drain of their healthy green hue. Through slim holes in his camouflaged position, he had a narrow view of the open ground before him. Twenty meters to his front was a large oak, with a small knot of purple-bushed leaves accompanying it. Sam could clearly see a student hiding in the bush who had thus far, managed to evade discovery.

Sam's friend Peter came into view. He was walking very deliberately, like a bloodhound on the trail of some wily fox. Peter's mottled dirty brown hair fell over his eyes as he plodded along. He passed the child hiding in the purple-leaved bush and walked past the tree, dismissing the area as a viable hiding spot.

Several feet away from him to his left, the bushes along the school wall shook. The bush was thick enough that he couldn't clearly see if someone else had also chosen the bush as their hiding spot, or if it were one of the seekers. He leaned forward, cautious so as not to reveal his position, but still couldn't see anything. He reached one hand onto the ground in front of him to lean a little further. As he did so, a hand reached in and grabbed his shoulder. Off balance, he fell forward in a heap, halfway out of the bush.

"Ah-ha! I've got you!" It was his classmate, Miranda. Her dark black hair fell in straight, long lines past her shoulders, her blue eyes shocks of electric ice. She hadn't let go of his shoulder, and the hand he had planted in the dirt gave way. They collapsed in a heap of dust and leaves, Sam twisting enough to land squarely on his back, the wind leaving his lungs in a loud *hoof!* Miranda laughed as she put her other hand on his shoulder, and propped herself up. Their eyes met and a weird spark tickled through his stomach. Without hesitating, she leaned down and kissed him on the lips. It was his first kiss.

He withdrew from the memory, and again noted the feelings associated with the memory melted away from him. He pulled his gaze back into the near, and turned to look at Armand.

The old man looked back at him with calm, reassuring eyes, then redirected his gaze back to the ocean. Sam followed, turning his eyes towards one of the storms in the distance.

The sea was an angry wraith. Waves shoved over one another, spraying whitewater in a cacophony of unending, reckless cannonades. The spray rained down on the recoiling water, and Sam was transported into a heavy downpour.

The loud patter of rain was maddening; it dominated the soundscape. He heard it in the thick grass on which he stood. He heard it smack off the stones that surrounded him, and how it broke through the frail umbrella of leaves overhead. He heard it as it fell in the dull, agonizing thud of freshly dug earth.

Sam stood in an open field, holding his father's hand. The rain tried to wash away the tears streaming down his face, but only served to reinforce them. His mother was there, but wasn't. She was in a box under the earth where they stood. His young mind frantically tried to find footing in the loose gravel of eternity. His mother had fallen ill, he'd been told. She lost so much weight. Diminished. The glow in her eyes, once so vibrant, turned hazy and yellow. Her skin, once warm like the sun, eclipsed into something pale and cold. Her cheek bones protruded as her skin became like cloth. And then, the end.

Something in his mind closed shut. His walks with his mother, done. Her greeting him in the morning as the sun rose onto his pillow, gone. He searched for a way around the barrier, searched for a future moment with his mother. She was there. But she wasn't. There was no path, no entrance. On a trip visiting family in a distant town, they had once passed by a castle, a relic of another time. Fascinated, he pulled away from his mother and father, racing to the side of the castle as fast as his little legs would allow. Panting feverishly from running up the hill on which the castle stood, he rested an arm against the castle wall, and looked up.

The stone wall, massive and indomitable, swallowed his entire field of view, so much so, he could hardly see the break of the parapet at the wall's top. Even looking slightly to either side, the wall yielded no relief, no invitation. Then, it had been fascinating. Now, the barrier that had sealed some part of his mind off was colossal and absolute. Death.

He withdrew his view and like before, the feelings from the memory, the wicked, confused and gnawing trembling that accompanied the crossing of this darkest threshold, evaporated from him. The process was slower this time, his breathing was quick, shallow gasps of air. Slowly, he came back to the tower on which he and Armand stood. His breathing slowed, and his voice sounded like a foreign thing when he spoke.

"What was that? What happened?"

"What do you think happened?"

Sam blinked to focus his eyes. He looked at the ocean, then back at Armand. "I saw moments. Memories of things that happened to me. But they were vivid. So real. I...*felt* them."

Armand cast his gaze down at his feet, his hands clasped thoughtfully behind his back. "What did you feel?"

"I felt...joy. Silliness, but boundless joy. Bliss. Then, excitement. Giddiness. Embarrassment and awe." Sam glanced in the direction of the storm. "Confusion. Unbearable sadness."

Armand walked to the edge of the tower and sat down. The wind was steady. He motioned for Sam to join him on the tower's edge. "Don't worry. You won't fall."

With some hesitation, Sam did as Armand said and sat next to him. When the old man spoke again, it was genuine curiosity.

Sam shook his head.

Armand leaned towards him, resting a hand on Sam's knee. When he spoke again, it was just above a whisper. "Your memories and thoughts are there, across these seas, these oceans. You 'see' them with your awareness. You 'feel' them because your energy follows your awareness. Did you notice, when you left each memory, whatever energy you felt receded?"

Sam nodded.

"If I tell you to think of the saddest day of your life, what happens?"

Sam drew his eyes to the storm he'd just visited. Like a rising wave, he felt the convulsive nausea from the storm rise around him. He pulled back from it.

Armand nodded. "And to the happy memory of childhood, barely old enough to walk?"

Sam searched the ocean for a moment, then focused in on the first memory he'd seen, with his mother and the bath. Giddiness bubbled at the shores of his awareness. He felt a smile coming on. Wherever he directed his focus, his energy followed. A spark of comprehension fired deep within him; the waters immediately around them tremored and flattened, triggered by the shifting of some seismic Faultline in his psyche.

"What was that?"

Armand laughed, a deep, hard laugh that turned over into a cough. "That, my young friend, was understanding."

The old man was right; it was understanding. It was an understanding that was sublime and ubiquitous. An understanding that rippled across his mind, might still be rippling for all he knew.

"I know this now." Sam said confidently.

Armand's eyebrows raised, furrowing his brow in deep, familiar lines. "Be careful. What does it mean to know something?"

Sam laughed, then looked at Armand with an expression of surprise, before giving way to laughter again. "It means...it means, I know it."

Armand raised a hand. "There are three levels of knowing something."

The first level, he relayed, was simple cognitive knowledge. "You read or hear something, you understand it, but you don't fully know it. If you try to apply it, invariably you come up short."

"I think I understand what you're saying." Sam said, pursing his lips. He wondered if the words came out more convincingly than they sounded to him.

Armand continued. "When you are able to act on what you know, you have achieved the second level of knowledge, emotional. At this level, you understand the consequences of your actions. Stick your hand in a fire once, you know not to do it again."

"And the third level?"

"Physical knowledge." Armand said matter-of-factly. "The knowledge is a part of you. You don't need to think, you just act. Think of the master sailor, who commands his ship, sensitive to the language of the ocean. He pilots his vessel with complete command, understanding its abilities and limitations. Riding the fine line between the two in what we call seamanship. So...tell me what you 'know'."

Sam, at Armand's behest, explained to him that his awareness had gone to the places of the mind Armand had guided it. A happy moment of youth. His first kiss. His mother's funeral. As he took his attention to each memory, the rapture, or the heartache, of the moment came into the light of his awareness.

Armand smiled thoughtfully. "Yes. Exactly. It isn't that you become those emotions but rather, you feel and sense the emotions of those moments."

Sam leaned back onto his elbows. "Those feelings were so strong. The memory of the funeral was so clear."

Armand leaned forward, stretching his back. "Emotional moments can create strong memories in our minds. People condition themselves, revisiting the memory over and over, until it becomes reflex. The feeling begins to control them, shaping their life. That's how patterns are created. Patterns of limiting beliefs. Most people don't realize they can control where they direct their awareness."

Sam bolted upright. "How is that possible? I have so many thoughts in my head. How can I possibly control them? How can I keep my mind from wandering?"

Now Armand leaned back. He rested a hand on Sam's shoulder as their eyes met.

"You still have much to learn." With that, Armand shoved Sam off the tower edge.

Journal Entry: I cannot say how it comes to pass that I make this entry; perhaps I have gone mad. Am I safe? I do not know. Is my journey over? I am unsure if it is even begun. The lighthouse was there, then it was gone. Perhaps it was never there, and I am in some padded room, lost in the seas of my mind. Even with these fanciful notions, I hope to capture the clarity of the discoveries made.

Our mind is like an ocean, full of the memories of all the events that make up a life, and full of everyone we've ever met. Our awareness is like a lighthouse. We can shine it anywhere within the ocean we choose, though most people let their awareness wander the way a lighthouse lantern circles the seas in its rotation.

We can learn to control where we direct our awareness through the three levels of knowledge:

1. Cognitive knowledge. We read or hear something, and we understand it. This is the limit of this knowledge in that, if we try to apply it, we find we cannot. While we comprehend the information, we cannot effectively put it into action.

2. Emotional knowledge. *At this level of knowledge, we can successfully apply action to our understanding; we can understand the consequences of our actions. If we call someone a bad name, and repeat it on seeing them several times, we see the effect it has on them and, realizing that we are causing pain, can cease using that name.*

3. Physical knowledge. *Finally, we act on instinct. Action is automatic. Innate.*

When we revisit memories or actions, we create patterns. These patterns create habits. These habits become our lives. If we are not careful, we can create habits that are not healthy. Some patterns become such a part of our life, we are hypnotized by their rhythm. Think of the lonely man who instinctively reaches for a drink after every day's labor, or the person who shuffles their feet uncomfortably when they are the center of attention. These patterns are sometimes the hardest to break, and must be replaced with a strongly felt, new pattern.

PART TWO

THE
STORMS
WITHIN

CHAPTER FIVE
THE MONSTROUS ROGUES: THE SEA OF REGRET

Sam fell. At least, that was the immediate sensation he felt after Armand pushed him. And even that memory was slipping from him the way the last drops of water leave an overturned cup. Falling was the best description, given the circumstances.

The world was complete darkness. There was airflow over one side of his body, which reinforced the sensation of falling. He wasn't accelerating, not that he could tell. Nor was there the sense of impending calamity or impact.

And then lights. Bright, flashing coils of light that arced around him in wild, fantastic loops. Brilliant blues, oranges. Yellows and greens. Reds that gave way to pink. Even with his eyes closed, he felt their color. Felt the varying degrees of their warmth.

The airflow shifted or rather, he shifted direction. He tuned into his sense of equilibrium. Whereas a moment earlier, the idea of "down" had been at the crown of his head, he now felt it from his chest. Not falling. Flying.

The air passed over his face in warm caresses. He wanted to open his eyes but found he couldn't. The idea itself, this transitory blindness, was not altogether unpleasant. The lights racing around him were comforting.

The airflow slowed. "Down" assumed its normal feeling beneath him. He felt pressure against his butt and legs. The lights withdrew, replaced by something else. A different light. There was the sound of water lapping against something solid. He opened his eyes.

He was in a rowboat, similar to the one tied to the dock. *Perhaps the same one*, Sam reasoned. He was wearing the same clothes he'd been wearing in the lighthouse, but something was different. He felt his head. He hadn't been wearing his watch cap, but it was on now.

The air had the pleasant, distinct smell of wet wood. For a brief instant, he thought of the smell one finds when opening an old wooden box. What he now smelled was a cousin to this smell, and equally as pleasing.

He held oars in either of his hands, facing astern. At the back of the boat sat a young boy. He wore a simple brown shirt, with darker brown pants. Curls of hair escaped from underneath the boy's black cap. The boy looked at Sam and smiled. It was the telling smile of one who held a devilish secret close to his chest.

The grey-purple sky was a fleet of quick-moving, bloated storm clouds that grumbled and belched in unchecked anger. Judging from the deep, imperial blue of the ocean, Sam surmised they were far out to sea. There were wide, cavernous troughs between the waves, giving him the feeling of being in a valley of water. A very perilous, wide valley.

Sam looked to either side of the boat, struggling to remember how he came to be in this place. Then in a rush, whispered secret, it came to him. Armand had pushed him. Falling and flying. Where was he now? And where was the lighthouse? So many questions. And the boy.

As if on cue, the boy spoke. "Hello Sam."

Sam looked at his companion. He looked familiar, and yet Sam knew he'd never met the child before. He guessed the boy to be no older than ten, and had the immediate impression that the boy was odd. He sat upright in the back of the boat, hands neatly folded in his lap. His clothes, his face, were all disturbingly clean, and he seemed out of place in the choppy ocean waters sitting in the back of an aged, fatigued rowboat.

"How do you know my name?" Sam asked, followed immediately by, "Who are you?"

The boy responded nonchalantly. "I'm you."

Sam stared at the boy in disbelief; it wasn't like staring into a mirror, or looking at a photography of his younger self. From what Sam could tell, the boy's hair was darker and cleanly trimmed then Sam's had been in his younger years. His features were clean; the boy lacked the small mole Sam had under his left eye, his nose was narrower, and his shoulders seemed broader than Sam's had been at that age.

A strong breeze blew across the boat from starboard, and it became clear. The boy looked like a neater, idealized version of how Sam had wanted to see himself when he was younger. The unblemished face with the reduced nose, the stronger shoulders, all aspirations he had held for himself when he was younger. Something in Sam understood that the boy represented a physical manifestation of his mind, a caretaker on this strangest of journeys. The realization brought Sam a sense of comfort.

"My mind is full of so many things. Do you represent all of it?"

"Just the waking part," the boy offered.

Sam started rowing. He had no destination in mind, but he sensed that moving was better than sitting still, especially as the waves grew increasingly menacing. "So, the conscious mind?"

"Yes."

"Is there another version of you for my subconscious mind?"

The boy frowned. "No. I am the gateway."

"What does that mean?"

The boy moved. He shuffled to the port side of the

boat and dipped his hand in the water. He held it there with his index finger leading and watched it, a small rudder gliding calmly through the ocean's churn.

"The subconscious mind is objective," he said without looking up," I am subjective. It takes whatever it is fed. Then it acts on it."

Sam smiled, "Ah well. It would have been neat to meet the both of you."

The boy kept his eyes fixed on his hand, cutting through the water.

"Well," Sam said, smiling at the boy, "I can't call you 'Sam'. That would be strange. How about my middle name?"

"Joseph it is," the boy replied.

So, Joseph...what is this place? Where are we?"

Joseph said nothing. Sam looked around.

It was hard for him to see over the walls of water that surrounded them. The boat undulated on lesser waves, but never rose above the distant peaks. He couldn't discern if there was land near them or not. Joseph raised his hand from the water, pointing over Sam's shoulder.

There was nothing. Only water. Then a wave caught them, the boat rose and he saw it. A speck of light really, at an extreme distance. A lighthouse. The image flashed briefly before being gulped down by a wave. But Sam knew what it was. In this little boat, it would take hours to reach, maybe a full day. The lighthouse appeared again. It stayed visible longer this time. He kept staring at it before coming to a realization. The lantern from the lighthouse was fixed on their location. He turned back to Joseph.

"Is that...?"

Joseph nodded. "That is where you were. Now you are here."

Sam released the oars, letting them hang in their outriggers. "And where exactly is here?"

"Before I answer, I must tell you something. There is another here."

Sam stopped rowing, and leaned forward. "What do you mean, 'another'? Is Armand here?"

Joseph shook his head, his eyes widening slightly, "No. Another mind."

"Something beyond the conscious and subconscious mind?"

"Yes."

Sam looked back in the direction of the lighthouse. After a moment, the boat rose and he saw it over a wave crest. "What is it?"

"I don't know."

"What do you mean, you 'don't know'?" Sam whipped around, stirring the boat, "how is it possible that there's something here you don't know."

Joseph's eyes widened further. Fright lit his face momentarily, bringing a tremble to his lip. Whatever was behind it vanished, and calm returned. "I don't know."

A large humpback whale breached less than a

hundred meters from them, its massive black frame reaching a near-horizontal plane with the surface before it flopped down onto its side, sending torrents of water raining down.

Sam looked in the direction of the impact. After a minute, the whale's back rose out of the water several meters from where moments before it had crashed down back into the deep. The whale was still or, Sam reasoned, moving with the same current they now rode. He guessed the whale was curious about their little boat.

"Is that whale the 'other mind' you speak of?"

Joseph looked at Sam with disappointing eyes, and shook his head. "I don't know. I just know this is a place of sorrow."

The weather was worsening. A steady rain came at them sideways, and stinging saltwater spat at them, carried off the wavetops by emboldened wind gusts. Lightning flashes created an eerie bluish glow in the leftover foaming bubbles from crashed waves.

Sam had been rowing at a steady clip. He regularly waited for the boat to rise on top of a swell before looking behind him. They had been pointed towards the lighthouse for most of the afternoon, and Sam intended to keep it that way. It made sense to him, and there was no other sign of land to guide them. The weather didn't look like it was going to break anytime soon.

At the same time, there was a duality at work he didn't fully understand. From the tower before Armand had pushed him, his gaze had lit up any area to which he looked (*like a lighthouse*, something inside him offered). Now, he was on the water, ostensibly *his mind*, rowing back to himself. With his mind his only passenger. He expected the idea to create nausea, but there was none. Not yet.

Joseph had become more serious, eyeing the water in all directions, though they hadn't seen the whale, or anything else for that matter, for a while. He was ruminating, wrestling with unspoken tensions. After a time, he spoke.

"These waters make me think of an old man."

Sam looked up, somewhat surprised by the comment. "Which old man?"

"There was a man from town. He lost an arm. Some kind of industrial accident. He could never get over what happened. I remember seeing him, stumble about town, blind-drunk and reeking of alcohol."

"I recall that fellow," Sam offered.

"I remember father said the man drank. He drank because he thinks if he had done something differently, had left work earlier, or later, the accident might never have happened."

"Yes," Sam interjected, "He drank to numb the pain. To

forget. And then he would sober up, and be right back to wishing things had turned out differently. But he doesn't want to drink, because somewhere deep in his soul he knows he is wasting his life."

Joseph didn't make eye contact, and his shoulders drooped slightly. His eyes fixed on something in the water. "We all have regrets."

"What are you talking about?"

Joseph's eyes widened. "Wave!"

Sam turned in time to see the sky blink closed from an enormous wave bearing down on them. There was no time to turn the tiny boat; the wave might be ten meters high or more. He felt himself pitch back towards Joseph as the boat veered up the wave face, and only managed to keep himself seated by bracing his feet on the deck and the oars against their outriggers.

The bow cut through the wave crest before it broke and for a brief moment they floated precariously in open air until the boat slapped back down into the water with a loud *SMACK!* Sam's teeth rattled with the impact.

They were now heading down into a trough.

"Keep the boat pointed into the waves or we'll capsize." Joseph cautioned.

"What? Capsize? Get us out of here then." Sam implored.

"I can't. I don't have that power."

"You've got to be kidding me," Sam exclaimed, "what do you mean, 'you don't have that power'?"

"This place makes me sad," Joseph said, "a memory won't release me. And you're holding the oars."

Sam tried to process what the boy had said, but more immediate matters demanded his attention. He knew there was no point in switching places; Joseph was small and couldn't manage the boat as well as he. The rain was heavier now, and cold.

The boat rose on a small wave. Sam turned and looked behind them. The distant speck of the lighthouse beckoned. Even well-rested, it would take hours to reach. He wanted to rest. He dropped the oars and sought to refresh himself by splashing his face with saltwater.

Inexplicably, an image of his mother came to him. It was a moment altogether familiar to him; a moment he had revisited almost daily since her passing.

He was seven, an age when the wonders of life were as plentiful and as breathtaking as the sea of stars that sprinkled into the sky over their house with every day's ending. That particular day had been as so many were back then; lush with joy, rich with laughter. School was out, and the earth was still in thoughtful balance between the hesitant warmth of spring and the domineering furnace of summer.

He was with his family down by the stream and, only now, looking back on the memory, did he understand how much his mother loved that place. She didn't just love it because of the mesmerizing sound of the water, or the spacious cocoon afforded them by the wreath of trees that opened themselves so generously to a spot as sweet as this. It was sublime, but what called to his mother was something more meaningful. This place, in all its beauty, was theirs.

The journey, the reclamation, had taken time. Time, patience, and sweat. His father liked to say, 'saltwater cures everything...the sea, sweat, or tears...take your pick.' As a young man, Sam had always found the saying kind of mystical and neat. After this day, it had taken on a new kind of meaning.

They started claiming this place by moving large rocks and deadwood, and then setting medium-sized rocks on either side of the dirt trail that led from their house, to make a trail. He and his father went about the work eagerly and, though young, skinny, and small, Sam felt like he was a genuine partner in the effort, not some child given token tasks while his father did the real work. It was bonding on a level that was simple and straightforward. A bonding that, after his mother's death, would grow in a vein of necessity that he always struggled with. It was unnatural, and yet it was the new order.

They had dinner at home that day, then his mother suggested a walk to the stream. Ten minutes later, they were there. His father diligently inspected the tidiness of the place, while he removed his shoes and splashed along the stream shore.

Earlier in the spring, a storm had ambled through,

with dazzling flashes of lightning and ear-splitting thunder cracks. The storm rolled right over their modest house, and the next day they discovered a bolt had struck down one of the larger evergreens on the far side of the stream. It left an ugly hole in what had previously been a uniform line of treetops, standing like sentinels over their sacred place.

The body of the tree had splintered and twisted violently, leaving it with the surreal look of an oversized stick that had been wrung by some angry giant's hands. The top three meters of the tree had ripped completely off.

The treetop had fallen on their side of the stream, with nearly two-thirds of it now in the water. It wasn't damming the stream completely, but Sam could see the debris and loose limbs bunching and starting to interrupt the flow. In time, it could choke and flood their little piece of paradise. His father tried to lift it to no avail; that led to a discussion between his parents on getting someone to help. In the end, his father had settled on the intention of cutting it and then hauling it to the house to use during the next cold season.

The light had grown dim, with the sun dipping well into the tree line. The evening was coming on with its hallmark soft shapes and lines. Sam was tired, and when his father said it was time to head home, he was the first one to head towards the trail.

Sam had been playing on the swollen side of the

stream; it was now forming into a shallow cool bath. As he splashed out of the water, he heard something rustle underneath the fallen treetop, but paid it no mind; sleep was winning the tug of war with his consciousness. The night creatures were beginning to stir, and a symphony of crickets and frogs were seeking their own harmony.

He waited by the foot of the trail until his father joined him.

"Your shoes." His mother reminded him, as she gathered the last of her things.

"Go grab 'em." His father offered, patting him lightly on the back.

Sam took a step forward and made eye contact with his mother. "Can you get them? I'm tired."

"Where are they?" She asked, looking down at her feet.

His arm felt heavy. Too heavy to lift. He managed to raise his hand, and pointed to the tip of the fallen treetop, a few feet from the water's edge. His little brown shoes sat huddled together like small little wood creatures. The thought was fuzzy and scattered, and made him smile.

His mother walked over and bent down to grab the shoes, only to quickly recoil, gasping as she did so.

His father rushed to her side. There was a muffled, anxious conversation between the two of them, with his father stomping his work boots into the ground. The speed at which his father moved, the tension in their voices, jolted Sam from the harbor of sleep he had been sailing into. His father picked up Sam's shoes, placed one arm around his mother and hurried them towards the trail.

"What happened?" Sam heard the cracking uncertainty in his young voice, the erosion of his fatigue now fully unseated by a tentativeness that was a child's introduction to true fear. The urgency that sizzled in the air now shot a tremor of anxiety from his groin up into his throat.

His mother looked at him, her eyes wide in a way he hadn't seen before. It was a strange look; one of surprise his younger self thought. But Sam knew better. It wasn't surprise. It was sorrow.

They passed him, and he turned to follow. He glanced back to where his shoes had been, straining to make sense of the darkening woods, the deepening shadows. He wasn't sure, but thought he saw something orange and yellow.

The familiar serenity of their house was turned into a swirl of frantic chaos. His father hurriedly helped his mother into bed. There, she convulsed in painful tremors as coughs rattled her body. Sam's father directed him to get her water, and declared he was headed to town to get the doctor. Within minutes, he was out the door.

Sam drew a cup of water and stood in the kitchen. Silence. Perhaps his mother had fallen asleep. He felt his heart pounding in his chest, throbbing into his throat. Then, a stillness came over him. Even reliving the memory, he wasn't sure what it was; it felt as though some thing had entered not just the house, but his world. One minute the air had been free of it, the next it was saturated with an unseen heaviness. It wasn't humidity, but a wave of something. Something unpleasant. Something like—

"Sam."

Her voice was clear. Calm. He heard nothing else. Not his heart. Not the water spilling over the cup lip onto the floor in his shaking hands. He stepped towards her bedroom. Towards her voice.

He walked on weak legs through the doorway. The air smelled wrong. There was something sickly sweet, and damp.

She lay there, looking out the window in the blackness of night. She looked so different. His mother. This woman who had nursed him, bathed him, soothed him when he was hurt, tended to him when he was ill—that person was evaporating before his eyes.

She was motionless. For a second, he thought she may be sleeping with her eyes closed. Then, another thought crept in. It was a horrible thought, elusive and gnawing in its incomprehensibility, a thought that scrambled across his psyche and just beyond his understanding like some devilish, manic spider. He couldn't identify it, but it terrified him. The thought scurried away into some dark, webbed recess when his mother blinked and turned to him.

Her eyes brightened momentarily, the way a dying fire finds a brief reprieve in a dry leaf.

It was her eye contact that kept him from crying out, from screaming. From her eyes, he saw her beauty. Through her eyes, he saw his mother, in all her infinite and unconquerable brilliance. Fixed on her eyes, he did not have to focus on the yellowing creature, drenched in sweat, whose very essence seemed to be shrinking before his eyes. He had the nauseating feeling of being a tightrope walker in the circus, balancing across some unbearably deep chasm. Her eyes kept him from looking down into an unspoken madness.

Before he knew how, he was next to her bed. She managed something like a smile and coughed, then raised a hand to his cheek. Her touch was like white-hot fire, and he shuddered at the heat coming from her. Concern bloomed weakly across her furrowed brow. When she spoke, her voice was weak and uneven.

"I love you, son. I'm glad it was me." The words sounded other-worldly. Sam looked at his mother like she was speaking in a language he had never heard; it was her voice, ragged and thin, said in a tone that might be used with a stranger. A fierce coughing fit wracked her body, convulsing her nearly upright. She looked suddenly frail and skeletal. He stepped back, afraid.

The coughing fit left. She managed to drink some of the water he had brought her and, finding an incredibly reservoir of strength, lifted herself off the bed far enough to kiss him on his forehead. She muttered something about rest and for him to go to bed. He meekly obliged.

His sleep was dreamless and deep, and had been the kind of sleep most associated with exhaustion. When he finally woke, he was greeted by the full light of day. He heard his father's voice in the other room, answered by the muted sounds of a stranger's voice murmuring agreement. His mind reassembled the events of the previous night and whisked him back into the present. Perhaps his mother had fully recovered, and they were discussing what to do with what looked like, by all accounts, a glorious day.

He leapt from his bed and raced to his parents' room.

His father stood at the foot of the bed facing it, hands on his hips. On the right side of the bed, a round man stood. His hair was cottony white and well-combed, and his cheeks full and round, contrasted by the thin lips that formed his mouth. He was dressed in a long black coat with a pristine white shirt. The man nodded, looking between the bed and his father.

Sam's mother lay in bed, her skin, so fiery hot and red/yellow last night, had paled. Sam thought it looked blue. She was looking out the window, as she had been last night, but Sam saw that the light had left her eyes.

"My god," Joseph cried, tearing at his hair with his hands, "it was meant for me. I should have been bitten by the snake. It should have been me!"

"What? No," Sam blinked. They were back in the boat, which was being battered by increasingly bold waves. "You didn't...we didn't –"

But Joseph's sobs stopped him. The boy buried his heads in his hands. Another wave, slightly smaller than the previous rogue, barreled toward them. They took the wave at an angle, the tiny boat see-sawing as water splashed at their feet. The trough they fell into was deep, though Sam hardly noticed. He felt himself sliding into the despondency of his companion.

"You can't think like that," Sam pleaded, "you must let this go."

"I can't," Joseph managed between sobs, "I killed her!"

"Of course you didn't. You did no such thing."

"I did."

The trough was deep because the wave building towards them was gathering energy. It was becoming a mountain of water. Sam took his attention from Joseph and turned as the boat began riding up the face of the wave. He saw the wave start to break; it snarled at him with rabid whitewater which flew from the crest like spit from the mouth of some charging sea-wolf.

There would be no cutting a path through this colossus; that much was clear to Sam. The wave strangled their tiny boat. Its indomitable claws held them as they went vertical before overturning them, consuming them in a wall of ocean.

Sam felt weightless as the boat ejected him. There was the curious sensation of floating in space. Then, he was underwater, upside-down. He clawed for the surface, but found only water. His lungs began burning; he hadn't had time to take a breath. Flashes of lightning flickered overhead, before the sky went dark, the water, black. He reached through the darkness and found wood. The boat.

It was overturned. He managed to prop an elbow on the boat's exposed belly. Above the water, it had gotten dark; he could barely see, save for the flickering illuminations of the awakened storm. Splashing to his right. Joseph surfaced a few feet away.

Sam released his hold on the boat and paddled over to Joseph's flailing arms.

"Hang on, I've got you." Sam said, spitting out gulps of water. He grabbed an arm and tugged the boy towards him. Joseph didn't struggle. The boy in tow, Sam turned and saw the silhouette of the hull. With his free hand he scooped through the water until it was within reach. "Grab onto the boat."

Joseph did. The boy's face was a veil of anguish. It was as if he was oblivious to the change in their circumstances. He bit his lower lip as tears mixed with sea water flowing down his face.

"Killed her." He cried into his sleeve.

Sam felt a strange tug from the left. It was another wave building.

"Joseph, please. You can't think like this."

His words were lost on the wind, as the next wave picked them up. Sam had the comical notion that this wave would knock everything back to the way it had been moments ago; they would end up inside the rowboat upright and intact.

Instead, he found the darkness of unconsciousness.

Consciousness came back in fragments. Sam was displaced. Was this real? Why was everything so hazy? There was the sound of a whale exhaling. Darkness. The warmth of something smooth and the wooden tang of the boat. Somewhere in the distance, his consciousness thought it heard the sound of water hitting land.

Journal Entry: I cannot tell you how these words are transcribed. They are not written in my journal, for it isn't with me. This is some strange kind of other-worldly record keeping. Some heavenly plane perhaps, outside the normal rules of time and space. How am I writing, or am I only imagining this? Is it in my mind? Am I? If so, there is no trace of my erstwhile companion, Joseph. Joseph, my mind. Perhaps he is lost; I stagger at the implication of, if true, what that must mean for me.

He/we are a prisoner of the past. I see that now, and have always known it. I have created this confining room of debilitating belief about my life, my responsibility for what happened to my mother. And, even as I have grown... physically, spiritually, emotionally and mentally...I have unfailingly managed to discomfort myself into staying in that room. It has cost me so much already. Driven by blinding fear and unshakeable feelings of inadequacy, what have I lost? What have I missed out on? Countless treasures, and immeasurable trials, for no life is free of heartache. But what I've really missed out on is growth.

This story no longer serves me. I need to write a better story and then let it go. If I keep telling myself this story, continue to live in the past, how can I focus any energy on the present, or build a good future?

I must find a path to wresting control from Joseph, assuming he is somewhere to be found.

CHAPTER SIX

THE HARROWING SHALLOWS: THE SEA OF COMFORT

The distinct and inviting sound of waves crashing along the shoreline was the first thing Sam became aware of. There was the rippling gush of water hitting land, its momentary and ill-fated charge up a sandy beach, followed by thousands of tiny gurgling chimes as shells flipped end-over-end with the water's receding. The next wave rallied like some determined cavalry commander, gathering the scattered remnants of the preceding wave and stormed the beach again, and over again.

Next, he smelled green things. Plants. Trees. The scent of something citrusy flirting with the bite of salt air. He heard wind through leaves, and not in a hurried, stormy sense. It was steady, low-talk similar to the trees near his home, barely a noise but something more than silence. Finally, as his senses fully returned, *the sun*. Its heat and warmth nudging him, like an anxious dog, nosing for attention. He felt it on his back, prodding him back to consciousness, felt the contrast of its warmth against the cold damp of his clothes. He instinctively licked his lips and tasted sand.

Wiping his mouth and opening his eyes, he blinked repeatedly to make allowance for the brightness of the day. Jolly, puffy white clouds drifted in scattered clusters across brilliant blue skies.

Sam had been laying face-down ten meters from the shore. His eyes struggled to make sense of an object on the beach. Then, he recognized it; their rowboat. The boat was upside-down on the beach, its bow burrowed into the sand. A gaping wound on the port side promised the boat would not again be sea-worthy without significant repairs, the likes of which he doubted would be found close by.

He pressed himself off the ground and looked behind him. A lush green jungle was close enough that he could hear monkeys chattering back and forth, their small, dark shapes darting between branches. Wondrous palms held huddles of coconuts. He sat up.

Before him a little to the left stood a small, thatched hut. It sat atop four thick tree stumps, with three wooden steps leading up to its entrance. The hut's opening faced away from where he sat, but he sensed no one was presently inside. Immediately to his front, meat roasted on a stick over an open fire, it's sparks dancing up into the sky. Smoke drifted away from him in slow, swirling tendrils. In front of the hut and meat, a lagoon beckoned, its intense turquoise waters glittering like jewels in the midday sun. A coral reef interrupted the beach to his right. It ran in an arc in front of him, a natural border between the ocean and the lagoon, before bumping up against a wall of trees on his left a short distance away. The shore of the lagoon came down the reef/tree boundary and made a nice sandy crescent that curved in front of the hut before ending in the mass of coral to his right.

Sam stood and walked past the hut, not bothering to look inside. Instead, he stepped to the lagoon's edge. To his left, two white-crested oystercatchers made sweeping trails around the shoreline, frantically chasing fast fiddler crabs that raced into their homes in the sand, too fast for the birds' beaks. Beneath the lagoon's pristine waters, there were mountains of vibrant coral. The lagoon's current had arranged the sand in even rows of white, brown, and then white again.

He saw sea urchins nestled in their little crevices in the coral, their needling spines swaying gently back and forth. Schools of tiny fish, royal blue in color, glided between pillars of coral, as larger yellow fish with black stripes probed along the sandy surface in search of food.

Joseph stepped out of the jungle, cradling an armful of fruit.

"What happened?" Sam asked. "I remember my mother, then there was the wave. It swept over us. And then..."

Joseph made his way over to the hut and dropped his collection of fruit near the steps. He looked ragged; his hair was a mess and there was a tear in his sweater near the left shoulder. "And then we ended up here."

"And where is here?"

Joseph didn't reply. He sorted through the fruit before settling on a small melon. He grabbed a nearby rock and hammered it against the skin until the fruit broke.

Sam looked at his companion, then back to the lagoon. "My mother. I still feel her. The feelings. They haven't gone away like before."

"She's with me everyday," Joseph offered between bites, "I carry her with me everywhere. I carry so much. I wish I hadn't killed her."

"We—you didn't." Sam said in his best reassuring tone. "That snake..."

The boy did not relent. "I should have picked up my shoes. That snake bite was meant for me. I know that now."

Sam had grabbed a piece of fruit for himself and sat on the steps, rolling the fruit back and forth between his hands. There was a truth in what Joseph said. It was a line Sam had told himself over and over again, without ever really debating the idea. Now, it had become a belief. A belief that was so ingrained and such a part of him. How would he ever shake it from his mind? Then, inspiration struck.

"You're right." He said.

"Of course I am." Joseph said matter-of-factly, juice running down his chin.

"The snake should have bitten us. I, we should have died."

"Yes, instead I carry this guilt. It does not let me go."

Sam paused in his eating, turning his gaze to the lagoon. "If the bite was meant for you, the snake would have bitten you."

"It should have bitten me," Joseph sniffed, "should have. My shoes."

"But that's my point. It would have bitten you if it was supposed to. It would have bitten you when you took your shoes off, or when you came out of the water. Then you would have died. You...we wouldn't be here. It is really as simple as that. And had that happened..."

"What?" Joseph asked, wiping his mouth and raising an eyebrow.

The thought struck Sam like a wave might a toddler in the shore break. It slammed against his psyche and he tumbled from the force of it.

"Mother would have been heartbroken."

A fierce wind rushed from the tree line towards them. It shook the branches and their leaves, as the palm tree fronds *shushed* in whispered agitation. The wind hit them; Sam could feel it, like a schoolmate tackling him. He braced himself as the wind roared passed them and went out to sea. Sam gathered himself, and looked at Joseph. The boy's face was calm.

"You're right," Joseph said, his voice clear and free of the heaviness it had just recently carried. "She would have anguished every day for the rest of her life. She would relive my death with every sunrise. The place that had been such a heavenly calm for her would have become a place of dread and torment, and she would tear at her own heart that it had been me and not her."

"Yes. Yes, that's it." Sam was dumbfounded. The truth had been there, a better belief in front of his eyes the entire time. An echo of something Armand had said lingered just outside his understanding. What had it been? What had the old man said?

Sam didn't quite understand how, but he was famished. The aroma of the cooking meat had started his stomach grumbling.

They ate, neither talking but instead focusing on filling their bellies, as the sun stretched further west into the late afternoon of his mind's sky. Feeling full, Sam had questions. Where were they now? How much time had passed? Where was the lighthouse and, most importantly, when would he return to the real world?

Joseph had gone into the hut and retrieved an axe among other things and, with Joseph standing on his shoulders, they were able to wash down the meat with coconut water retrieved from nearby trees. Sam rinsed his face in the lagoon water. Was there fresh water on the island? Another good question.

He wanted to approach Joseph with these questions, but the boy had fallen asleep leaning against the hut. Undeterred, he set out on his own to find whatever answers he could.

The island had everything he could imagine; it was a fine part of his mind. He reasoned that he would spend as much time in this area when he got back to himself. There was an abundance of fresh fruit. He had entered the jungle in the same spot Joseph had exited earlier and found there were all manner of trees and bushes with delicious berries, melons, and bananas. Besides monkeys, he heard other creatures; there were birds he'd only read about in books. Somewhere close by, he heard the squeal of wild pigs.

He hadn't wandered very far from the lagoon when he came across another surprise and an answer to one of his questions; a small spring of clear fresh water. *A natural spring*, he thought to himself, *this place is incredible.* He bent down and cupped some of the water in his hands to drink. It was cool and sweet.

There were rough, discernible paths in the jungle, made by the pigs he'd heard earlier, he guessed. Sam turned right to what he sensed was north, then checked the position of the sun, which was cutting through the tops of the trees to his left as it fell into the evening sky.

He was vaguely aware of the ocean waves to his right, which meant the hut was that way. After several minutes of making his way through the dense vegetation, he came to the northern edge of the island, where the trees met the coral reef that separated the lagoon from the ocean. The waves rushed into the reef, which was low enough that water glided over it in sheets, feeding into the otherwise serene lagoon waters.

The reef was wider in some parts than others, but easily traversable. He walked east to the point where the reef turned south towards the beach and stopped to survey the ocean before him.

The ocean rippled with subdued, dormant power. The look and feel of it reminded him of the seaside town he'd departed from on his way to Black Eagle. Compared to what he had experienced in the rowboat, the waters looked accommodating and even a little pedestrian. They put him at ease. He looked out further to his left; there was nothing on the horizon. As he scanned to the right, he saw it. The lighthouse.

The lantern was lit and focused on this, his island paradise. As had been the case before, he could see further than seem possible in the real world, and knew the lighthouse was at least as far away as it had been when they were in the rowboat. It was a strange sensation, this telescopic vision, and for the first time, he felt a little nauseous at its use. He kept scanning to the southeast, when something nearer the shore caught his eye. It was a flash, like one might see when the sun hits a mirror the right way. The sun was well below the island's tree line, and the waters where the flash came from were in shade.

There was something bobbing up and down perhaps a hundred meters from where he stood. It looked like a brown raft of some kind, but seemed too small, its edges too distinct, its shape too boxy. *Not something*, he corrected himself silently. *Some things.*

There was the larger boxed thing, but trailing behind it a series of smaller yellowish-white objects drifted in a loosely scattered trail. He followed them, allowing his eyes to sharpen as they drifted into the distance. There were hundreds of them, thousands even. He felt the nausea coming on strongly, but the smaller objects seemed to be leading back to the lighthouse.

The boxy thing was drifting closer to the island, and a stiff wind stirred, blowing more of the yellow objects from its top. Sam realized they were pieces of paper. *Like a journal*, something inside him offered. He blinked and looked at the brown box again. *A desk.*

Something by the desk flashed again, and this time he was able to center his attention on the area of the flash, but could see no objects. It flashed again.

Sam saw himself. He looked a little older than he presently was, and smiled in a childish, pained way at the fitful, patchwork beard his older self was trying to grow. There was a young woman with him, though her features weren't clear to him.

He was tripping over himself with excitement, walking in front of her, darting from side to side, hands gesturing wildly as he talked.

Sam could make out none of the words his older self was speaking, but understood the scene readily enough. The young woman was hesitant, but attentive. She followed him with her eyes (*what color were they?* he insisted to no avail), and frequently her gaze lingered long enough where she would catch herself. She would then gracefully look down on the path they walked. He thought her hair blond, but the vision was unclear. It fanned coolly off her shoulders, like curtains stirred by an evening breeze. She did her best to measure her smiles, so as not to convey enjoying his company too much.

For his part, Sam sensed his older self in love. It wasn't a love of hopeful anticipation, or short-lived fiery passion. It was a defining love. A love that would alter the flow of his life, become his life. And somewhere within him, he felt pride well up. Pride in seeing this version of himself recognize such a thing at an early age.

The thing in the water flashed again, and he held a bundle of cloth. He was older, and yet the spotty beard on his face remained. Why was he persisting? It was a terrible look. He laughed at himself.

A tiny, pink arm reached out of the cloth. His older self brought the bundle closer to his face, and the little hand found one of his eyebrows and instinctively clenched into a fist. *Better that than the beard*, Sam mused, his laugh coming back harder now.

A little boy with cropped blond hair rumbled into view, crashing into his older self's leg. The boy reached for the baby and said something in that same unrecognizable chime Sam had heard in the previous vision. The boy was followed by a man, who readily shook older Sam's hand. Both men turned, the stranger pointed at something Sam could not yet see. Finally the woman, the same one his older self had been fawning over, came into view. She carved a smooth path between the men and kissed his cheek. In one hand, she carried a book. She held it up, waving it back and forth with pride and excitement. As she did so, clarity came to him, and he saw his name on the book cover.

Sam pulled back from the vision. He bolted over the reef, skillfully navigating the cracks and potholes like a crazed ballerino.

The light was leaving the sky fast now, and as he neared the end of the reef, it became harder to see good footing. The campfire still burned bright, fed and stoked by some unseen hand.

Joseph was no longer outside. As Sam got closer, he thought he could hear the boy's heavy breathing from within the hut, where candlelight made odd shadows that danced lazily on the walls.

The dreams, or visions. The woman, he knew, was his wife, the children, his children. The book. His. He wanted to wake Joseph. To share the news, the revelation of the thing. This place, whatever part of his mind it was, was magical.

Fatigue caught up with him, and though it was only dusk, Sam stepped into the hut and fell onto the cot opposite the boy's. As sleep came for him, he was thinking about the vision. He drifted into sleep, imagining himself peering through a hole in a wooden fence. Then, he lifted his head and saw he could see above the fence. It was a silly thought, and yet the last thing he sensed before sleep was the unmistakable spark of discovery.

A sound woke Sam the next morning. He wasn't immediately sure what it was. The first idea that came to him was that he wanted to write. As he tuned into the day, he heard the familiar crash of waves rippling down the beach. There was the shrill chatter of birds, accompanied by the boisterous whooping cries of the monkeys. Closer to the hut, there was the distinct sound of chopping. A quick scan of the interior told him Joseph was already up.

He glanced outside and saw the day was just beginning; a breeze swirled inside the hut, a promise of the warmth to come. As he rose from his cot, something scurried across the roof, and his eyes darted up in mild alarm.

There was a blur of motion in the doorway as whatever had been on the roof dropped down and scampered to a nearby tree. The blur turned out to be a small monkey; it was covered in dark brown hair, save for a splash of ivory fur surrounding its face. In its tiny hands, the monkey clutched Sam's watch cap.

"Hey! Give that back." Sam shouted as he jumped down the steps. The monkey raced halfway up the tree to his front, turned and smiled a toothy grin, then leapt for the nearest branch, where it sat triumphant.

"You mongrel. If you're part of my mind, I command you to come down and give me my cap."

The monkey chittered, then began picking at the watch cap as if plucking fleas off a friend.

Sam looked for something to throw, before deciding against it. He was thirsty, and recalled there was a jug of water next to his cot. The monkey could wait, and the weather was warm enough where he wouldn't need the cap anytime soon. He went back into the hut and sat down on the cot.

He poured himself a cup of water and drifted back to what he had seen yesterday beyond reef. The pages in the water and image of the woman. His family. His book. It excited him, awakened something inside that he had put to rest in recent years. He had set aside any dreams of writing when he left school. It simply hadn't seemed like a realistic way of making a living, not when so many of his classmates were pursuing what he thought of as 'real work'. And his father had deterred him. He remembered in particular a conversation he and his father had shared while extending the fence line of their property.

Snow had fallen. It was a rare occurrence where they lived. This snow was robust; when the last flake had settled, it was up to his waist. He spent breakfast standing next to the window, marveling at it. It changed the landscape so dramatically. The bleak, bare landscape of brown and grey was reborn in the pristine white stillness the snowfall produced. Sam was actually excited to be outside, until he felt the sustained presence of the cold.

The wind carried with it the bone-gnawing bite of humidity, and he felt it nibbling at his fingertips as they worked. He was wrapping wire around a fence post, while his father labored to get the posts seated in the frozen ground. The older Seagrim, wanting to help pass the time, asked his son how school was coming, and what he enjoyed the most.

"Writing," Sam had offered, fighting off the urge not to curse as the wire chewed into his dry fingers, "I like it. I like telling stories."

His father had chuckled.

"What's funny?" Sam asked, the wire digging deeper. He could see a blossom of blood open on his index finger.

"Nothing." His father grimaced as he put his weight into the post in his hands.

Sam had wrapped the wire five or six times around the post already, but pulled the end in his hand. He pulled with enough strength that the post shifted slightly towards him. The wire strained in his grip, and the blood from his index finger deepened into a rivulet that trickled over his thumb.

"I want to know." He demanded.

"The people who write are professional writers", his father huffed, "they have a gift, and hone their craft".

Sam released the wire. He looked at his father. A wound opened somewhere inside him. Not unlike his cracked fingers, it too bled. It was something he couldn't verbalize and nothing he could point to. But it was there, bleeding. Gushing. Shaping his world in ways he wouldn't immediately appreciate, but only begin to accept as the scar healed and he, in turn, healed into something else. Something different. He left the wire and walked towards the house.

His father called to him, said something that was lost on the wind.

And that had been that. The idea had been shelved.

Sam came back to the present. He drank the water, cool and refreshing. He thought of the pool he'd seen in the jungle. He wanted to further explore this wondrous place.

Joseph appeared outside the hut, dragging three evenly-cut pieces of wood. The boy wore pants and an undershirt; the sweater he'd worn on the rowboat was draped over a bush near the tree the cap-stealing monkey had climbed. Sam judged the pieces of wood to be just less than three meters each. He marveled at the boy's strength; the wood looked heavy.

"I thought the fire didn't need tending." He mused.

Joseph wiped sweat from his brow and entered the hut, grabbing his own jug of water. "The fire? No. I've been thinking about regret. About the things we talked about."

"Oh?" Sam was surprised, "And what have you concluded?"

"Well, if we view things as happening "to" us, we might always feel like a victim. If we view them as happening "for" us, we might take away some kind of lesson from them."

Sam was delighted. "What did you learn about regret?"

Joseph took another sip, then wiped his mouth on his arm. "I guess...to be grateful for the time we have with people. That, if everything happens for a reason, try to learn what the reason is. And that nothing is really gained by focusing on regret, except sorrow."

"Regret is a bottomless jug." Sam said, sitting next to Joseph. He sounded like Armand. The idea suited him. "No matter how much you pour into it, or drink from it, the jug never empties. Sorrow can be a blessing, if we understand it."

"Yes. And, not thinking about my mother in that way doesn't diminish my love for her."

"Why would it?" Sam asked.

"I don't know why I thought that. I guess it's just a question of telling myself a different story."

"Now we're getting somewhere."

Joseph offered a curious look to Sam.

"That reminds me!" Sam exclaimed.

He went onto relay what he saw while on the reef wall the day prior, the desk floating in the water, the papers floating around it, and the woman and children. He mentioned the book with his name on it.

In reply, Joseph offered that what Sam was seeing was what he truly wanted from his life. That he was gazing into the sea of dreams. Sam was pleased by this. This led them to a discussion about how best to address the fact that they were stranded.

They would need to build a raft to get off the island. While Sam slept, Joseph had been busy. He had surveyed the row boat and found the damage was as bad as it appeared; the boat would not get them off the island. On a brighter note, he had recovered both oars.

The boy had found a grove of saplings on the other side of the pool of water. They spotted more than a dozen that were dead or dying, the wood drying, and cut down six; he estimated they might need five or six more, along with vines to twist into rope to keep the wood together. They would build their raft.

Feeling energized, Sam agreed to the plan; Joseph would find the vines and begin making rope while Sam would take over and finish the job with the saplings. The two set off into the jungle.

They made good progress. By the afternoon, they had turned the beach into a makeshift workshop; Sam had dragged the dozen cut saplings towards the water and had them neatly aligned into the skeleton of their raft.

For his part, Joseph had found an enormous tree deeper into the island; its trunk was twice as wide as their hut, and the tree mushroomed up through the jungle canopy so high the treetop disappeared from sight. Thick, wild vines of green and brown shot down from its limbs like the impossibly long legs of some giant creature. Joseph learned that some vines pulled down from the tree more easily than others. Some were easily strong enough to support his weight. He wanted to climb them. Once the raft was built, he would show them to Sam to see if he wanted to have some fun before they departed the island.

They stopped work when the sun fell into the trees to the west, and the air cooled. Sam had finished with the tree cutting by midafternoon, and had used his time to manicure the saplings, cutting off fledgling limbs and assessing which pieces fit best together. That finished, he then worked on intertwining the strips of vine Joseph had provided, fashioning them into the rope that would hold their raft together.

The next day, after a breakfast of fruit and coconut water, Sam took Joseph to the reef point, where he had previously seen the visions. As they walked over the coral and sand, he noticed the tide was out; the waterline was lower on the reef, and wasn't splashing over the surface like yesterday.

It was a desk, today that was very clear. The desk bobbed in the water, with wet pieces of paper scattered around it, and the trail of papers leading all the way back to the lighthouse. The woman and children were there in shimmering luminescent ripples. Sam asked Joseph is he saw them. The boy replied that he did.

"They are so close." Sam squatted down, leaning over the coral's edge, "I want to get back to real life. Surely seeing them so close must mean these things will happen soon."

Joseph casually looked at the visions in the water. "Yes, it would be good to find this out."

By noon that third day, the raft was complete; they had more than enough rope to secure it on the ends and through the middle, and leftover wood as well. They piled the wood next to the hut, where it would be partially protected from the rains. They lifted the raft up to test its resiliency and were pleased to find their bindings held the raft together tightly. A quick test in the lagoon affirmed the raft sea-worthy, capable of holding them both and whatever supplies they saw fit to take with them.

Sam was anxious to leave, suggesting they cast off after getting a good meal in their bellies, but Joseph preferred to wait until the morning.

"The day is half over," he reasoned, "we surely won't make the lighthouse before it's dark."

Sam thought about this. He wanted to get going, but perhaps the boy was right. They could start fresh in the morning. He pulled the raft from the shoreline, and tossed the oars on top of the raft.

"This will give me a chance to find that monkey and my cap." Sam stated.

As Sam wandered off in search of the cap thief, Joseph went into the hut to determine what they could take with them on their journey.

The next morning greeted them with a downpour. The rain came down in misting, defiant grey sheets the obscured the far side of the lagoon. Thankfully, the roof of their hut was substantial, and rain only spattered in by the hut entrance.

After much searching the day prior, Sam had found his cap at the foot of a banana tree just inside the jungle.

The rain brought with it considerably cooler temperatures, and he wore his cap as he stepped to the hut's opening.

"Today is lost."

They agreed to gather up what supplies they could from the hut. Joseph had taken smaller pieces of wood and some of the leftover rope to make a small crate, which he suggested might be used to take both their water jugs with them. Along with the jugs, they would take the hand axe, a knife, and some extra rope if they wanted to try their hand at fishing, or if they needed to anchor or secure the raft. Of course, they would take as much food as they could, both fruit and some of the meat.

After several hours alternating between light chatter and fitful sleep, Sam grew restless.

"Why can't we just leave? Can't I snap my fingers and come back to the real world?"

"Why can't you?" Joseph asked, feigning interest. He lay on his cot, arms folded behind his head.

Sam shot the boy a perturbed look, then snapped his fingers.

Nothing.

He frowned. "What was it you said to me the other day? I should enjoy the moment or something. Then that is what I shall do."

With that, Sam threw himself down on his cot, closed his eyes, and went to sleep.

The rain lasted throughout the day. With the sun setting deep into the tree line, the storm finally broke. The air dried, pulling the standing water back into the atmosphere.

When they woke the next morning, the eastern sky promised better weather. Sam was up before his companion, and fastened the crate onto the center of the raft, the thinking being that they would be on either side paddling, and the supplies would be in easy reach whenever one of them was in need. The tide was low, and he pulled the raft closer to the water's edge in anticipation of their departure. By the time he was done, Joseph was up and finished eating. He came over to where Sam was sitting, having just gotten the raft into position.

"Before we go, there's one more thing I want to do."

Sam stared into the waves, without looking at the boy. "Oh? And what's that?"

"You must have seen the tree where the vines came from. It dominates the jungle. I want to climb to its top."

Sam couldn't stop the frown from curling onto his face, but Joseph didn't relent.

"Besides," he said, "it will give me a better view of the island. And the lighthouse. To make sure we have smooth sailing."

"Well then, that sounds something worth pursuing." Sam responded flatly.

Joseph looked at him, and then nodded in agreement. "Won't you come with me? Then we'll go."

Sam got up, and the two of them headed into the jungle.

They didn't make it to the top of the tree, but got close enough to feel a sense of accomplishment. Even high above the jungle floor, the limbs of the tree were thick enough for them to stand. The tree tops to their east obscured the hut, but Sam had a sense of where things on that side of the island were. To the west, the trees dropped off into a valley, revealing a cove with a hill on the far side that looked like a giant ant mound. The waters of the cove looked as appealing as those of the lagoon. Joseph wondered aloud what they might find on the far side of the island. Assuming there wasn't anything beyond the western hill, the island itself didn't look large.

"I bet we could circle it in one day if we started early enough." Joseph offered.

Sam was silent.

They returned to the hut with the sun still high in the sky. Both were hungry, and readily ate more than they had allotted for. Recognizing this, Joseph offered to gather more fruit to stock their journey. Without waiting for discussion, he went off into the jungle. By the time he returned, it was later in the day.

Sam did not offer conversation as the day slipped away. As they settled into the hut, the evening was still, the tenants of the jungle quiet. Only the single candle burning within the hut offered any kind of motion, its light swaying calmly.

He felt apprehensive, knew of a tension building between them. Finally, after a long period of silence, he spoke.

"You want to explore the rest of the island."

Joseph broke from his daydreaming. "How did you... the far side of the island looks worth exploring. That's all."

Sam didn't move. He lay on his cot, his hands resting on his stomach. "You saw the dreams, didn't you?"

Joseph sat up. "I did. They're close. We should be able to catch them in no time."

"Our dreams are just on the other side of the reef, waiting for us in the waters. So close, you can feel them. Isn't that what you said? And yet, what are you doing?"

"There are other things we needed to do."

Sam bolted from his cot and stood in the center of the hut. The candle convulsed in a wild frenzy, sending dancing shadows across the hut's interior. When he spoke, he was calm, but his words carried the heat of the nearby fire.

"Are there? A watch cap? Climbing a tree? Seeing the island? What's next...let me guess. There's a cave on the far side of the island. When we explore the island, we'll explore the cave too. You're wasting time."

"I am not."

Sam now moved to the hut opening. The night was thick with the sweet smell of coconut. "Of course you are. You're afraid. And your fears keep you here. Finding reasons to stay. Excuses to avoid starting the journey."

"I...there are sharks in the water. I...I've seen them."

"Sharks?" Sam laughed, "What are you even talking about?"

Joseph stood. "Please...just one more day. The other side of the island might tell us something important about our trip."

The boy walked past Sam out into the night. He trotted past the fire and leapt onto the coral reef, taking it down until he sat, his silhouette outlined by the shimmering glow of the watery dreams.

Sam thought of how relaxed he felt in this place. How at home. It gave him pause to reflect on his own life and how many times comfort had caused him to hold back, to not take opportunities or risks. Moments in school. In relationships. Romance. Moments of his life. All because his mind found some loophole to talk him out of doing the thing he wanted to do.

He looked back at the candle; it might last another hour. It was time. He knew it, even if Joseph didn't.

Sam leapt up and grabbed a handful of dry straw from the roof of the hut. He stepped down next to the leftover wood from the raft and crammed the straw into the cracks and crevices. From there, he went back inside the hut, grabbed the candle and carried it outside, cupping the flame to keep it from going out.

The straw welcomed the flame. Sam feared the wood might be wet from yesterday's rains. The burning straw soothed the wood. Caressed it, inviting it to partake in its dance. Finally, the wood accepted. It caught fire, and excitedly spread, crackling embers up into the night's sky. Some of the ember's floated up into the underside of the roof, where they lit.

The hut itself started burning easily. As it did, Sam realized he needed to grab everything from within the hut they needed for their trip. The heat was growing quickly, and the interior of the hut was filling up with smoke.

He got what they needed and carried it several feet away from the hut. He was putting down the blankets when Joseph came racing up to him.

"What have you done? Where will we sleep?"

Sam looked at the boy, then to the hut. The flames were shooting up into the starry night. Some of them had managed to leap onto the fronds of the nearby palm tree, which then started burning. It was possible the entire island might burn. Sam smiled. *Hopefully.*

"You never told me the name of this place, but I think I know it." Sam said, still admiring the hut. "We leave tonight. Now."

And so they did.

Journal entry: How many times do we allow fear to talk us out of doing the things we most want? How many occasions do we fall back into the welcoming arms of comfort, only to become entangled by its nefarious cousin, complacency?

Fears spin up inside us, coiling around our minds like a snake. We over-think. Over-rationalize. Until we successfully talk ourselves out of doing something, and think that solution is the rational choice.

There is no perfect time to get started. Perfection is the enemy of progress, and will defeat us before we ever start. Our minds will consume whatever we feed them. I keep coming back to what Armand said about there being only one master. I think I'm starting to understand what he meant.

CHAPTER SEVEN

THE SWIRLING ANGST
THE SEA OF ANXIETY

The waters were calm, placid even, under a waxing
moon that lit a path for them. Even in the glimmering
sparkle of the midnight waters, the dreams preceded
them. Sam remembered reading about the northern
lights; how particles of light from the sun collided with the
earth's atmosphere to create bands of light that waved in
enchanting, mystical streamers. That was how the dreams
now appeared. They weren't images like they had been
when he spotted them from the island. They were green
and purple hazy wisps that moved always out of reach, like
a desert mirage. As the lights moved, they absorbed the
floating pieces of paper that Sam knew would lead them
back to the lighthouse. Back to reality.

For its part, the raft was a sturdy thing. The top
side was surprisingly dry and, while the ocean's mild

temperament hadn't proven to be any kind of test for it, both passengers felt it would hold up if the weather turned on them.

There were no immediate signs of fatigue, none that either of them let on. There were only the visions, and the lighthouse. These two things, surreal and yet real, were intertwined, like the shreds of twisted vines that held their raft together. They paddled in the mysterious and always-shifting direction of the floating lights. They stopped for a bit, and let the ocean take them, both stirring with hunger. Sam finished his food before the boy, and used time to fasten the remaining rope they had into a kind of lasso. He toyed with securing a piece of food into the loop and tightening it down for bait, but quickly gave up. The rope was too big, and a big piece of food might bring a big kind of fish. Maybe the kind they didn't want around.

No words were exchanged between them, nor was any attempt made at conversation. Sam, filled with nascent purpose and growing confidence that he was taking control of his mind, rowed with a growing obsession, captivated by the possibilities before him. Joseph glanced at him occasionally, but stayed silent. There was the sound of the oars cutting into the black waters, the timid lapping of waves off the front of their raft, and the labored breathing of their efforts.

Sam watched the moon set, as the hours of darkness stretched on. He wondered where, exactly, it set to. Was there an edge to his mind? Did he have a doppelganger somewhere on the other side of the world...when the moon set here, it rose in that person's mind? Were all minds somehow connected? The question made him feel queasy.

As they paddled, they stirred up the most brilliant blue algae. It swirled in hypnotic, electric blue spirals before trailing behind them in their wake. The algae's bioluminescence made Sam feel like he and Joseph were on a magic carpet, floating along over serene air currents. The stars above them felt closer, their journey, more meaningful.

He stared into the blue glow, broken up occasionally by the silver flash of the fading moon reflecting off a wave. A wave caught the moonlight, and Sam blinked. When he looked again, there was a whale underneath them, gliding past their raft. Its body was clearly visible, and lit up in the glow of the algae like an otherworldly behemoth. As it passed, it gave a flick of its tail, sending the algae into turmoil.

Sam was transfixed. He saw the algae, then saw into the algae. He saw the tiniest particles of substance, smaller than he should ever have been able to see, saw these tiny bits dance around one another in some cosmic orbit of natural law. He saw deeper into the infinitesimally small physical substance, saw the energy of these particles. So much energy.

The particles of energy connected with other energies, forming larger particles that took the shape of miniscule twigs, twisted together. *Twisting* together. They grew larger still, then slowly began to resemble a recognizable shape. He had the curious sensation of watching algae being born. Then something even odder happened.

A tiny protrusion, nothing more than a nub at first, grew out of the algae. At first, it poked straight out. Then, after a moment, it began wiggling, frantically trying to free itself. It shook back and forth violently and did break free. It wasn't shaking anymore. It was swimming. A fish. It grew tall yet flat, turning the same fantastic blue-green that the whale had been. Then it flashed its translucent orange tail and swam into darkness. Something else broke free from the algae. It too shook in rapid fashion in order to free itself. This object looked like a coin, Sam observed, except it was a coin that bent nearly in two. The center thinned as the edges of the coin elongated; a butterfly. The nubs were popping off the algae rapidly. There was a deer. A shire horse. A sparrow. A woman. A lion, all the same blue-green as the fish and the whale.

Sam couldn't turn his eyes away. He saw planets form. Moons and suns. He blinked.

They were all gone, all but the coils of glowing algae corkscrewing behind them, the cloud vapors on their cerebral voyage. Whatever he had just witnessed, he knew it was the "other" mind Joseph had mentioned when they first met.

He looked back at the ground they had covered, then to the path ahead. The lighthouse was little more than a dot on the horizon, but the light coming from it, shining toward them, seemed brighter.

There was no hint of sunrise; the night had taken on the air of a secret, even forbidden thing, and Sam sensed it must be very early in the morning.

"What do you think –"He looked to Joseph, but the boy was fast asleep, his oar held in his arms, one foot dangling over the raft edge.

Orange. Orange and red. He tasted the colors before he saw them, if such a thing was possible in this place. Before consciousness fully embraced him, he heard his father's voice in his head. *"Red sky at morning, sailor take warning,"* his father had offered on one of their first trips to the coast. It meant a storm was coming he was told, as his father pointed out to him the red sky in the east. The rising sun reflected off the undercarriage of the clouds in the morning sky, which suggested the storm was moving towards you. The saying had a much-sought after counterpart, *"red sky at night, sailor's delight"* which alluded to the same thing happening with the clouds and the setting sun, meaning the storm had passed.

But something about this sky was different. It wasn't

just the clouds that were red; the sky was too. Redder, and more orange. The hues were invasive, not content to stick to the underbellies of the clouds. Sam had seen the sky like this once before.

It was a time when the seasons were changing. His mother had been gone almost a year. He wore her absence like a heavy coat; it rounded his shoulders, and his neck craned forward under the weight.

It was not yet evening, and the sky had become the color of rust. At first, Sam thought his eyes were playing tricks on him. Green bushes were green, but stained a hazy burnt orange. From where he stood outside the chicken coop, the house looked like a mad artist's dark rendition of their home. Even the chicks that scurried about on their tiny feet were an odd, off yellow. There were clouds, but no rain. Only the next day had his father told him of a tornado that had touched down on the opposite end of town.

Back in his mind in the present, Sam slowly came into his senses. With his fingers he felt the small pool of sea water that had found its way into the crease between pieces of wood. He was laying on his side. When he opened his eyes, the small puddle of water reflected an eerie reddish tint. As he pressed himself up, he knew they had entered a nightmare.

The ocean was scarred a terrible reddish-orange, like molten lava flowed on the surface...a fresh, untended wound. The stain was there in the troughs, and in the crests of waves. What had once been whitewater now foamed decidedly scarlet. *Like a sea of blood.* The thought assaulted his awareness before he could reject it.

"Joseph. What is happening?"

The boy did not immediately respond. Sam was struggling to understand how such a place existed in his mind. Such a wretched, tortured desolation. Even as he wrestled with the ugliness of this place, it felt known. Familiar.

He anxiously scanned the horizon, struggling to get his bearings, but a distant fog encircled them. Gone was the luminous algae that had made this all feel like a dream. Gone the floating, rhythmically gliding bands of light. Gone, the lighthouse.

"Fire Algae."

Those words, uttered from the parched lips of Joseph, gave shape to the sight Sam saw before them. He now saw texture and form. He saw degrees of color; this spot immediately to his left was a pale, sickly red, while up ahead there was a patch of arterial red. Through the vary degrees of color and densities, he saw the dead fish, floating on the surface, their nerves crippled by this awful red tide.

He wished to be away. Far away from this place. Away from his mind. Back in the secluded confines of Black Eagle lighthouse. Back home. Far away from whatever terrible logic had given life to this place, this terror in his mind.

He started to say something to Joseph, but stopped himself. The boy's eyes were wide with terror.

"Joseph!" Sam shouted. The boy looked at him, never losing the wide-eyed fear. "Paddle."

With the variation in color and density their only frame of reference, they paddled into the less dense, lighter patches of fire algae. Where were his dreams? Were they gone? A ripple of fear raced through his spine. What had they done?

"I'm not good enough to be a writer." Joseph said, tears coming to his eyes. "Even father knows it."

Between his sobs, the boy started laughing. It was a fitful laugh, an odd and discomforting 'uck'ing.

Sam's mouth fell open. The energy of the boy's words slammed him like a wind mashing a loose shutter against a window. The smell of the dead fish reached him, and he repressed the urge to vomit. This place was foul. The doubt and anxiety of failure hung in the air. Sam dropped a hand into the water, wondering if he would "sense" what Joseph was thinking. As his fingers entered the sea, sparks of electricity rocketed up his hand into his arm. The air on his forearms stuck straight up, and his claw clenched shut.

He wasn't good enough to make it as a writer. He never had been. That was why he never wanted to share his writings with anyone. This woman, this family that had danced before him, offering him a sip of joy the likes of which he had never known, would never want him. Father had been right.

These thoughts assaulted his senses and yet, even as they did, he recognized them. These were the stories he had told himself time and time again. He had never mustered the courage to believe he could make it as a writer. Had never believed in himself. And even though he had never met the woman in the visions, he had told himself a safe version of that same tale; he would never be good enough for love.

Sam pulled his hand from the water, and the thoughts dripped down his fingertips back into the sea. He stared at Joseph with amazement. He sensed the worst; he was losing the boy.

"Even father knows it." Joseph said under his breath. He had stopped rowing and was hunched over, his chin nearly resting on his chest. And he continued with the mindless, alarming "ucking".

These thoughts and the emotions they carried had been with him since his mother died, and he had told himself these lies, invested belief in them, until they'd become a part of him. They were his beliefs. They were *him*.

Uck-uck-uck...

Beyond the sound of the water hitting their raft and the boy's staccato laugh, there was another noise, faint but distinct. Sam recognized it instantly. It was the sound of waves crashing against rock.

There was a flash in the air, like lightning. Sam waited a moment, anticipating the grumble of thunder that would follow. He waited. Nothing. The flash came again, rippling through the fog like a—

"Lighthouse!" Sam shouted, "Joseph, it's Black Eagle. We're close."

Joseph looked at him, but said nothing.

"Uck-uck-uck..."

They had cleared the fire algae, but now found themselves inside the fog.

Even with the algae behind them, the fog had the tinge of that same rusted red. It was a thick fog, the air was hard to take into his lungs. Ahead of them, something loomed. Something massive and steadfast. Within the thick murk he could make out shapes, craggy sentinels jutting out of the ocean to greet them. Somewhere beyond a taller, dimmer shadow emerged. As he looked on, the familiar flash of the lighthouse lantern whipped over them from the top of the shape.

"Joseph."

"Uck."

Sam leaned into the center of the raft. He grabbed Joseph by the shoulder and shook him.

"Snap out of it!"

Joseph's eyes met his. He *ucked*, blinked, then blinked again. He grabbed Sam hard.

"Don't you see?" The boy shouted, "Father was right. Real writers have a gift. They hone their craft. The wire hurts my hand. It bleeds, it bleeds. I'm not good enough. What happens if I fail?"

Sam felt the pain in the boy's voice. The words from his father rolled over him like a cold spell. *The people who write are professional writers, they have a gift, and hone their craft.* He knew that Joseph, and by clear extension he, had accepted these words as truth. As a verdict, a judgment.

Sam recalled the moment in his mind. Felt the cold, biting wind, felt the burning fire of the wire in his hands. Walking away from his father and then his father calling to him. He had heard the words, but had not comprehended, kept the words separate, because he had already created a box, a limiting belief.

"You can be too. If you put the time in."

Exhilaration.

"Joseph, that's not what—" Sam stopped. The boat was turning. No. Not just the boat. The water. It was twisting.

To his left, the ocean was starting to flow away from them. There were no waves; the water pulled in long lines, away from them, circling to the left in a slow counterclockwise fashion. But when he looked to Joseph's side of the raft, the water was doing the same thing...except in a clockwise direction.

Like cogs in a machine, they were between two whirlpools turning away from one another, moving on unseen gears that brought their currents back together somewhere well behind them in the dense fog. Chance had, up until this moment, kept them centered, preventing them from being pulled in one direction or the other.

The sound of waves crashing onto rock was louder now, and Sam could see whitewater hitting at the base of rocks ahead of them. They were twenty meters from shore. The combined churn of the opposing whirlpools was steering them right towards it. In a few moments, they would make landfall.

Sam looked toward the center of the whirlpool nearest him. It was gurgling, sucking the fog down into it as it did. Remnants of red algae snarled into ragged bands that circled the vortex, constricting into ever-tighter coils until they were sucked down into the black center. There was something else in the center, but before he could make it out, he heard the loud crash of water hitting the rocks in front of them.

Sam recognized the spot instantly. It was a small inlet on the island; the dock was located on the island's far side. There were three enormous rocks that guarded the back of the inlet, closest to the lighthouse. Armand called them the three wisemen, as they resembled wandering nomads rising out of the dark waters. The shape of the lighthouse was plainly visible, and Sam thought he could hear the gears moving as the lamp rotated. He would need to oil his awareness when they made land. The thought brought a childish smile to his face, and he allowed himself to giggle. This strange, fascinating journey was coming to an end.

As they came into the mouth of the inlet, their progress was stopped. The water receding from the rocks was gushing out towards them, keeping their raft from advancing further, even as waves crashed around their now stationary raft.

Sam was sure if they could paddle, they could get past their watery impasse. He looked to Joseph.

The boy was turned away, completely fixated on the maelstrom on his side of the boat. Sam sensed they were past the point of being pulled into either of them, but felt the best thing he could do now was get the boy on land. He was still hunched over, and his fitful laugh had changed into a growling kind of hiccup.

To Sam's left, there was a large loaf-shaped rock five meters away. A sizeable piece of driftwood, the skeleton of some dead tree, had lodged itself at the base of the rock, its largest branch reaching up into the sky like a supplicant with arms uplifted. If he could lasso the branch, Sam reckoned they could pull themselves in and disembark there. He gathered the rope they had, stood, and threw the loop out towards the branch. The raft bobbed, but he didn't think they were in danger of capsizing.

His first and second throws missed, but with each miss, the rope got waterlogged and became heavier and easier to throw. His third toss saw the outer edge of the rope hit the branch. Finally, on this fourth attempt, success. He snapped the rope in his hands a few times, scooting the lasso further down the branch. When he felt like it was in a strong enough spot, he pulled. The noose tightened and held. The raft rocked for a moment before steadying, anchored to the island.

Sam let out a triumphant laugh. "Joseph, we made it!"

There was no response. When Sam turned, his relief turned to dismay.

The first thing that caught his eye was the boy's oar. He had tossed it into the water; the oar spun aimlessly before catching in the current of the far whirlpool. From there, it course-corrected, and began the increasingly-fast descent into smaller orbits around the center. As it grew near, the circles were too tight for the piece of wood to navigate; it knifed handle-up into the air before gyrating down into the blackness beneath.

Sam looked from the maelstrom to Joseph. The boy stood on his side of the raft, shins leaning against the basket in the raft's center, shoulders shrugged to his ears, his fists trembling at his sides. His face was a twisted mask of rage and fear. His bulging eyes were fixed on Sam.

"What if I fail? What if I'm not good enough? What if she doesn't love me?" Joseph spat the words from his lips, each question more distasteful than the one before.

"Joseph, please. We're here. We made it." Sam implored. The boy was beyond simple anxiety; he looked and sounded like he was on the verge of collapse.

Sam held the rope in one hand and reached for the Joseph with the other. They were slightly off balance now, but aided by the mooring to the dead tree.

"What if I fail?"

"We won't."

"What if I'm not good enough?"

"We are."

"What if she doesn't love me?"

Sam stopped reaching. He stood up. Joseph was crying now. He wanted to say something that would soothe the boy, but in his gut the truth came out before he could contain it. "Then, she doesn't."

"NOO!"

Joseph thrust himself backwards. He went headfirst into the churning water before surfacing and slipping easily into the clockwise pull of the whirlpool.

Sam rushed to the far side of the raft and leapt in after his companion, rope still in hand. He swam against the current towards the center of the maelstrom, hoping to intercept the boy as he circled around, until the rope yanked him back; from there he drifted slightly to his left before settling into an uneasy drag against the water's tugging. There was no more slack from the rope, but it looked like he was deep enough into the whirlpool to be able to snatch the boy.

Joseph was on the far side of the vortex, arms chopping at the water, eyes darting back and forth with fright. Sam watched intently. He estimated the boy would pass right in front of him; he turned back to look at the raft. It was gone.

Their combined weight had been enough to keep it in the purgatory between the landing and the sea; now that they had both abandoned it, the raft was slapping against the rocks at the inlet's deepest recess. As he watched, a wave fell right in front of it, shoving it into the three wisemen at the recess. The basket in the raft's center crumpled, and the force of the raft hitting the trio was enough to unsettle the ropes keeping the logs together. When the wave receded, the raft was a broken, ragged thing. Two of the logs were sliding out from the rest, and ribbons of rope dragged in the choppy water as the logs began to loosen from one another.

Another wave rolled in, lifting the raft back onto the wisemen, splintering it as the ropes ripped apart. Fragments of wood drifted uneasily in the waters, the skeletal remains of their salvation.

Sam looked back to the left to the driftwood and the rope wrapped around it. It looked steady and strong. As long as it held...

Looking back at Joseph, the boy was coming towards him. Sam realized he was farther in the maelstrom than the boy...his weight must have caused him to go closer to the mouth. He started grabbing the rope, pulling himself back towards the wood. The drag of the water surprised him with its strength.

Before he could brace himself or adjust, Joseph

slammed into him, horseshoeing himself around Sam's neck. Sam was completely submerged, and momentarily lost hold of the rope. He was turned around now, and felt them start to slide into the whirlpool's grasp. His lungs were beginning to burn, and he went to push Joseph's knees away from his face when he felt the familiar strands of the rope sliding over his fingers. Instinctively, he grabbed. The rope didn't immediately go tense and they continued to slide right when suddenly they jolted to a halt.

The force was strong enough to knock Joseph free, but he managed to wrap his arms around Sam's neck just as he surfaced.

"What if, what if, what if." The boy whispered mechanically.

They were now 'flying' in the water; their legs wiggled behind them in the current while Sam worked to pull them towards the driftwood. He had managed to move Joseph's arms from around his neck to his shoulders, enabling him to breathe. They made slow progress, one hand over the other.

Fragments of the raft were beginning to float by them. One of the logs that had first broken free was coming towards them; Sam thought it would float by them, and by the time it had made a loop around the circle, they would be past its orbit.

It passed by near enough to touch, but Sam was focused on pulling them forward. He thought they would clear the whirlpool in another ten feet, when Joseph lurched, reaching for the passing log. He grabbed it, and the log hurried on its path.

"Joseph!" Sam yelled, reaching for the log as it passed. His fingertips grazed the end but it floated on, now with the boy as its pilot.

Sam relaxed his hold on the rope, letting it slip through his hand as the current took him. He didn't have a sense of how much rope was free behind him, but knew there wasn't much. He was gaining on the boy, the alarm in his head growing louder as the rope snaked through his hand; he would have to let the boy make another rotation and catch him as he had before. He grabbed the rope.

He halted in a splash of water. His position was fixed for a moment, then lost more ground. He looked to the dead tree. The branch with the rope was straining against his weight but holding; the tree was beginning to squirm out of its lodgment. It shuddered, convulsed, and staggered away from the rock before halting. He jolted back a few feet, then stopped. It looked like the tree would be steady, long enough for them to –

Joseph slammed into him again. As he did, the tree broke free from the rocks and began floating towards them. Sam lost his hold on the rope. He moved his hand in the water, frantically searching for the rope. The tail of the rope snaked under the surface before his eyes. It was gone. He grabbed the log that Joseph was holding on to and they circled the vortex.

"Joseph, you have to do something." Sam pleaded.

"What if, uck...uck, what if."

Sam could see the mouth of the vortex. As they circled around it, he thought something was rising out of it. A mist or steam of some kind. Then the mist took shape. He saw himself.

He was not much older than he was now, and was sitting at a desk, pen in hand. This version of himself wrote, stopped, then started again. Suddenly, he threw his pen at the nearest wall and with his free hand swiped the paper from the desktop. It feathered and curled up in dying arcs before swooning to the ground. He buried his head in his hands.

The mist shifted, became just haze again, before taking new shape. Him again. Older. Squatting on the side of the street. His clothes were ragged and filthy, his face soiled and narrowed by hunger. He held a hat in his hand, rhythmically offering it up, greeting each passerby with a rehearsed, measured smile and woeful eyes.

Joseph grabbed Sam's jaw.

"Do you see? Do you see? Endless possibilities."

The mist, smoky and thick, shifted more quickly; one moment, he was failing to make a deadline for a newspaper for which he was working. The next, he was being rebuffed by a woman after asking her to dance. Then, he was at his father's funeral, so many things unspoken springing from his lips, hoping that his father now listened from beyond the veil. This version of him collapsed in a heap as his fellow mourners turned to walk away, only occasionally looking back on him with pity that, he knew, would leave them as soon as they left his sight. He saw chickens, so many chickens. The farm. His life.

Now he was aged. Liver spots dotted his scalp. He was in his family house, a physician standing behind him. He stared out the window, the same window his mother had stared out before she died. Sam looked at the vision of his older self, and their eyes met.

"I'm afraid you don't have much time left." The doctor said without emotion. He looked around the room, then checked his watch.

"There is so much more I could have done." His older self said, without adjusting his gaze. Then he blinked, sensed he was wasting the doctor's time, and dismissed him with a nod. The doctor gathered his things and exited the room. He looked back to the window, back to Sam. Their eyes connected again, and Sam thought, *knew*, that his older self saw him. Older Sam nodded. Then his eyes went hazy, reflecting on a past that never quite ripened. Finally, his gaze fell to the floor in defeat and resignation. The mist shifted again. There he was, an old man, crippled with age and impediment, lying in the same feeble, modest bed he'd grown up using.

They were nearing the mouth of the vortex, Joseph seemingly resigned to their fate. Sam felt them dipping downward into the darkness.

Something inside him awoke. It was a fire, racing through his nervous system, a tidal wave of energy and emotion. He felt it charge his legs and electrify his arms; an inferno erupted in his chest and up his neck. And he knew.

He knew that he had created all of this, knew that Joseph belonged to him, and the patterns, the meanings Joseph had assigned to experiences were of his making. He knew that he spent more time focusing on his fears and inadequacies than he did on his dreams. Finally, he knew.

Sam roared.

It was a roar that resonated throughout this world. The mist from the vortex and the surrounding fog receded then disappeared, revealing clouded blue skies overhead. Then the clouds retreated and dissolved. The swirling, hungry mouth of the maelstrom stopped, narrowed, and closed. The waters beneath them solidified, gently guiding their feet under them, and on to steady ground. The roar rippled across the ocean, stilling it, turning it solid, and the three wisemen collapsed, forming a rough set of stairs to higher ground. As he continued unleashing his soul, there stood the lighthouse, the lamp shining on them in brilliant ice blue light. He basked in the beauty of the lamp's warm glow, and became aware that Joseph was roaring as well. Sam looked at Joseph.

"I am the master of my fate." He said, his voice commanding and authoritative.

Joseph repeated the words, meeting Sam's gaze with his own. As he did, his complexion began to change, his form too. He was getting bigger, growing older before Sam's eyes.

"I am the master of my fate." Sam repeated the words. As he said them, Joseph matched his tone, and echoed the loudness of his voice.

"I AM THE MASTER OF MY FATE."

They were both screaming the words, the light from the lantern getting brighter. They kept repeating the words, Sam leading, Joseph following as they made their way onto the fallen three wisemen and into the lighthouse entrance.

Journal Entry: We can drive ourselves crazy, thinking about all the possibilities the future may hold. We can create endless anxieties thinking about the things we don't want to happen, and we only serve to give those things more energy and attention, increasing the likelihood that they in fact will occur.

We must focus our thoughts, our energy on the things we want.

PART THREE

SAILING INTO A DREAM

CHAPTER EIGHT
COMPASS OF THE MIND

Two blinks.

The first blink was when he stepped into the lowlight room, with its overwhelming brilliant, warm and shimmering light. When his eyes opened, he found himself in the rowboat on the waves of his mind.

Stepping into the lowlight room, he'd felt the fear bob into his stomach, the way a cork plunged underwater quickly resurfaces. Feeling that fear, the immediate thought had come to him, in the split-second his eyes were closed was one of recognition. He recognized how it had always been a part of him, always been there. Like some discontented guide, his fear had led him to make comfortable choices in his life. Choices that promised neither considerable risk nor meaningful reward. Choices that would lead him to the version of himself he met at the end of his journey.

Fear, in all its guises, had kept him safe. Yes, it put on the face of terror or panic when such responses were appropriate. But it also wore a false mask of courage to inspire him to perform, to achieve; a militant motivator. It wore the face of comfort, soothing him into the conditioning of creating a well-calculated, smart life. Calculated to deliver him to death's door neither wildly wounded nor clothed in the rapture of a life fully lived.

The second blink was when he closed his eyes as he and Joseph walked into the entryway of the Black Eagle Lighthouse of his mind.

The feeling that struck him as they walked through the door was galvanic and brought with it a surge of elation, unlike anything he'd ever felt before. It was like every hair, every ligament, every tendon, and muscle, even his skin, was super-charged with electricity. It was the intoxicating elixir of purpose. Of striving for something, a thing of focus that, by definition, scuttled other possibilities. Reaching for things perhaps not immediately within reach, and then growing into the person who could reach them.

As he opened his eyes in the present moment, a third feeling washed over him; a dizzying wave of nausea. He was back in the lowlight room, except now it held true to its name.

He found himself on all fours, and stood up too quickly. The uneasy wobble of sea legs greeted him, and he had to brace himself against the nearest wall.

"How is that possible?" He asked, blinking his eyes to see in the darkness of the room.

Armand stood in front of the closed door, his hands folded together. "How is a dream possible? In one night, we can dream a dream that lasts several years."

"So that was a dream? It felt like it. At the end. I...I took control of Joseph...my mind."

"It was like a dream."

Sam looked up from the wall and rolled his eyes. "It's good to know while I was gone you didn't lose your penchant for ambiguity."

"I am here to help." Armand replied dryly.

"Help...the man. The voice outside!" Sam replayed what had led them into the lowlight room in the first place; the cries of someone lost at sea.

He made his way to one of the narrow windows here and let his eyes adjust. Things gradually came into focus, but nothing stood out in the dark of night. There was the lamp casting its bright eye around the horizon, the occasional flash of a wave curling onto itself, and the glitter of moonlight off the water, but no man.

Armand opened the door to the room and walked out, offering, "The voice you heard was your own."

The next day dawned, and Sam woke with an altogether different feeling. His head was like a desert, not in the sense of being a wasteland, or being void of anything. On the contrary, he felt alive, invigorated, and fulfilled. His thoughts had a richness to them that was lush and nurturing. But in his mind, he felt shifting, like sand dunes writhing and flowing into new forms, guided by the invisible hand of enduring winds. He sensed his understanding of life and how he had viewed it up to this point was changing, morphing into new comprehension, beliefs being changed, and for the better. It made him smile.

They ate breakfast together at the kitchen table. Armand, content in silence, ate mindfully, savoring every bite, while Sam fidgeted and squirmed, picking at his food the way a bird might pick at a grub. It was the older man who finally broke the silence, much to the younger's delight.

"What is the biggest thing you learned on your journey?"

Sam started to answer, then stopped. It wasn't the question he had been expecting, if he had been expecting one at all. His thoughts were busy with writing, will telling stories, with the idea of love. There was an impulse he felt within to leave the lighthouse, but he tempered this feeling with patience. He knew he needed to know more.

To the question at hand, he reflected back on their journey. The waves that towered over them and brought them to the lagoon and then, finally, the whirlpools. He thought of the visions he'd seen and what they'd meant. Suddenly, it came to him.

"I am not my mind." He said it, and liked how saying it felt. "I am something else. I am soul."

Armand's eyebrows popped up, and he couldn't contain his smile. Sam continued.

"You said there can only be one master, but I think that has multiple meanings. In one sense, it means you either control your mind, or it controls you through the stories you tell yourself. Those stories imprison us."

"Is there another meaning?" Armand asked, wiping his mouth.

"Yes. What we focus our attention on. If we focus on fear, then fear is what we are creating in our lives. If we focus on what we want, then that becomes our creation. And even not wanting something to happen..."

He trailed off. Sensing his apprentice was still trying to make sense of things, Armand interjected.

"Think of this," he said, grabbing their plates from the table, "a man is barely able to make ends meet. He thinks he has just enough money every month to get by. But he thinks about not being broke, day in and day out, about not spending his money on foolish or unnecessary things. What happens?"

Sam shrugged his shoulders.

"He spends his money in the very manner he doesn't want to spend it. Because that's where his awareness is."

Sam pursed his lips, thinking. The old man had a head of steam and didn't wait for a reply.

"Now, the same man, same circumstances. A modest wage every month. Spends no time thinking about his money. Instead, he spends his time contributing to his town. He sees a beggar on the street and offers the man some bread. The beggar, touched by the man's generosity, tells his friend of the man's kindness. They too are beggars. The next day, there are three beggars there to greet the man on his way home."

"But the man is giving away all his bread. He will have to spend money to buy more." Sam responded.

Armand nodded.

"That may very well be true. He may have to buy more bread. But he is not thinking about money. Not thinking about all the things he doesn't want to waste his money on. And so he doesn't."

Sam leaned back in his chair, taking the front legs off the floor. "So if the awareness is on money and saving it or not spending it, it's one and the same?"

"Yes. Precisely. Not wanting and wanting are the same thing where energy and awareness are concerned. And both pivot around the same thing: not having enough. That is where the energy is really being focused."

"But then, how does the man make more money?"

"Ah." Armand said, delighted in the direction the conversation was going. "He asks himself a better question. The better the question, the better the answer.

A better question, control of your emotions...and faith."

"Explain."

Armand left the unwashed dishes in the sink and sat back down at the table. He took a long sip from his cup and continued. "Let's say this poor soul asks himself, 'how can I save every penny I make?'. His mind will provide him with an answer. Now, the answer may border on the ridiculous...it may cause him to deduce the best way to save 'every penny' is by subsisting on whatever food you have available, never leave the house, and enjoy only what nature provides for you."

"That isn't very realistic." Sam offered.

Armand nodded. "Quite right. Nor does it answer the question that you asked. This...is not a good question. A better question, and one that get to the heart of what you're after might be, 'how can I invest my some of my money to make it grow?" or 'what skills do I have that I can earn income from?'"

I like those questions," Sam quipped, "they make more sense. But what about emotion and faith?"

"Yes. Faith. If you believe in something, absolutely believe in it, how likely are you to see it through?"

"No question."

Armand drank the last sip from his cup and slammed it down with a satisfying ahhh. "If we believe we can do something, we will act with conviction. If we doubt, the effort we put forward will be laced with the seeds of mediocrity. Our efforts will not get us the results we seek, which will reinforce in us the middling belief that we were doomed to fail before we ever started."

"But how to have faith in something we've never attempted?" Sam asked.

"That is where control of the mind is key. We must visualize what we want. The mind is a tool; it will create whatever you set inside it."

"I think I understand now," Sam said, standing and stretching, "and with emotion...if I don't master my emotions, I will be a slave to them. That...that was what I knew at the end of my journey with Joseph."

He finished the dishes and left the kitchen to complete the morning routine. Sam made good use of his time, focusing his awareness on the task at hand, staying present, and doing his best not to let it wander to other things.

When he swept, he focused on sweeping. When his awareness drifted, and it did, he would tune into the sound of the broom against the stairs, and "pull" his awareness back into the present moment. He would this to be a useful trick; tuning into the sounds around him instantly brought him back into what he was doing. Sometimes, it might be birds; on other occasion, the hum or the generator, or the machinery rotating the lamp. When there were no external sounds, he listened to the sound of his own breath.

They finished the morning routine without interruption. During this time, a message came in from the mainland; Captain Stenson would be ten days behind in ferrying supplies to Black Eagle. The message said nothing more, and Armand was unfazed. They had plenty of food left and, while they were out of fresh fruit, they had vegetables from the garden room.

It was an unspoken understanding; Sam would return home when the Viaje made its next run.

Armand suggested they walk around the perimeter of the lighthouse. The waters were calm, and the sun had burned away the clouds, leaving only wide-open blue skies.

"So," the old man started, "there is awareness and there is the mind. Those are two points to guide you towards mind mastery. There are two more."

Sam took this in the way a drunk takes in their first drink of the day. He remembered when Armand talked about the disease of distraction, and his wooden catch-ball game. He thought of sweeping earlier in the day, when his mind had wandered then. If distraction had a polar opposite, it would be...

"Concentration. Focus must be one of the other points."

"Yes." Armand replied, quite pleased, "well done. And the last?"

At this, Sam stopped walking. He looked to the top of the lighthouse, then out to sea. He thought back to being in his mind. The whirlpools. What exactly had happened there?

He knew he had created the conditions, had trained his mind to react the way it did. His mind as Joseph wasn't crazy; it had only been operating on limiting beliefs. Beliefs he had invested in time and again. So what had broken the spell? Then, it came to him.

"Desire."

"Go on."

Sam walked back the way they had come, then turned and walked back towards Armand.

"When I was there, in my mind, and I saw how Joseph was a prisoner...how I had imprisoned him, and myself... saw a future of regrets and half-reaches. I didn't want that—"

"No." Armand interrupted him, but before the old man could finish, it was Sam's turn to interrupt him.

"I wanted something else. I wanted it so badly. So strongly. Something better. Something more."

Armand met Sam where he walked. The old man put his hands on Sam's shoulders and smiled. "You have done well, and learned a great deal. Now, you must find your why."

Sam managed a grin. "I understand these things, but they aren't a part of me yet."

Armand stepped away from him and sat on a nearby flat rock. He took off his shoes and socks, then removed his shirt.

"You know, it's such a pleasant day," he motioned to the waves, "I think I'll go for a swim."

He waded into the shallow water, then dove in.

Journal Entry: The quality of our lives comes down to the quality of the questions we ask ourselves. These questions shape, to an extent, the focus of our minds. Whatever questions we ask, the mind will invariably provide an answer. Poor questions, poor answers. Good questions, good answers.

Beyond understanding the relationship between mind and awareness, we must also understand focus and willpower. The better we are at focus and concentration, the better our results can be. The more we want something, the more we are pulled to it, the more our minds will find a path, make the path, towards its fulfillment.

As I watched Armand swim that day, I knew he was giving me the answer without ever having said it aloud. The way to make these things a part of me was right before my eyes. Immersion.

CHAPTER NINE
PATHWAY TO MASTERY

Meditation. The word had a curious air about it. It sounded of distant, exotic origins, and mysticism. When Armand first mentioned it, Sam thought of rooms, smoky with incense hanging in enchanted coils in the air, of low-voiced chanting echoing off stone walls. He thought of God.

He had tried it once, for a week, after a conversation with a classmate who was reading a book on Shambhala. The schoolmate, Cassandra was her name, had been fascinated with Shambhala, a mythical kingdom said resemble in layout an eight-pedaled lotus blossom encircled by snow-capped mountains. Her father had acquired the book on his travel as a buyer of jewelry and goods. The book itself was unremarkable in design or cover, but fascinating in content, or so Cassandra assured him. And Sam had to admit, the book smelled of cabalism and intrigue.

It catalogued one man's journey through Central Asia and into Tibet. In its pages, he chronicled the beauty and majesty of nature, exposing different aspects of Shambhala in the process.

The two friends sat together one day during lunch, her black hair draped over one side of her blouse, her dark, animated eyes following the pages she so excitedly shared. Cassandra had been particularly enamored with this idea of Samadhi—the idea that extreme concentration would lead to union with the divine. This concentration could be achieved through meditation.

He agreed with her that he would try it for seven days. Looking back now, he realized he was agreeing to it because of his complete adoration for her.

His first night was unsuccessful, chiefly because he attempted meditation while lying in bed, and soon fell asleep.

"You have to sit upright." Cassandra pleaded the following day. And so that second evening, that was what he had done.

His back grew achy as he sat on his cold bedroom floor, feeling a little silly. Soon, his cross-legged position became uncomfortable, and one of his legs fell asleep. All the while, he tried to clear his mind. He grew restless, switched legs, and alternated rolling his shoulders forward as he bent over to ease the stiffness seeping into his muscles.

By the fourth night, the aching was manageable, and he found a comfortable compromise in his legs that kept them from falling asleep. The 'clearing his mind' part was the challenge. In the book, which he skimmed through, it suggested to cease all thinking and just be. Then, the book suggested, after a time, a thought would 'pop' into his mind.

The problem was, the thoughts popped with irritating regularity, and without the "clearing" the author prescribed. He thought of what he'd eaten for dinner, of school work that needed his attention, he thought of scratching the itch that had flowered on the tip of his nose.

On day five, he gave the book back to Cassandra, politely informing her that he thought the whole notion silly.

While that had been just a few short years ago, the memory was fresh in his mind, and the feelings the word 'meditation' evoked were less than pleasant and vectored towards pointless.

"That's because you were doing it incorrectly," Armand stated firmly as they oiled and greased the lamp's machinery, "There must be a purpose in everything you do. Meditation is no different."

"Alright then, what's the way?"

No indifference, or even hesitation came from Sam.

After his incredible journey, he had come to see the old man as so much more than a lighthouse keeper, more than a teacher even. There was a deeper texture to the man; the very air around him seemed to crackle with energy wherever he went. The words he spoke came from experience, Sam knew, and those experiences had not so much shaped Armand, but rather had cut away who he wasn't, until he became the man Sam came to know. Even this realization would have been something that would have gone unnoticed just a few weeks earlier.

But this understanding was a part of him now, and it was continuing to unfold a new reality for him in the most wonderful of ways.

The energy of a person or thing was real, and there was good energy and bad. Thoughts were energy, and they too could be of a good variety or undesirable, and that holding something undesirable with his awareness would only serve to cultivate more undesirability. Focusing on good things would lead to more good things, which was not to say that bad things wouldn't happen, or would disappear from the face of the earth. Only simply, splendidly, that like attracts like, and seeing good or ill in the world came down to choice. Finding the higher, nobler truth of any situation would yield learning and growth. And when one held onto a thought or an idea for an extended period, that thought or idea could, would, manifest itself in a person's life. Burrowing further down into this rabbit hole, Sam reasoned that what someone believed about themselves, they lived. What he believed about himself would become his life.

The trick was, how to regulate this within his mind? Yes, the four points, the 'compass of the mind' as Armand called it, were key. But what was the path to making those points stick? The concept of mind and awareness had been easy enough to digest, and the journey they'd taken through his mind had cemented the concept as valid. How then, to make concentration and power of will, habitually reliable, to actually control and direct awareness?

They had finished the work of the afternoon and settled on the catwalk overlooking the ocean. The sun hung low in the sky, painting the western waters in fiery oranges and reds. They sat on the sunny side, taking in the warmth of the day, both pleased with the completed work and both eager to continue the discussion.

"Meditation has a purpose," Armand continued, his head resting against the lantern housing, "and the purpose of meditation is to use the energy within you, and the energy external to you. They seem separate, but they are actually one and the same."

"To use it for what?"

"To focus it. To harness it. When you talked of trying

to meditate on your bed...of course you fell asleep. We associate laying down with rest and relaxation."

"Isn't meditation meant to be relaxing?" Sam thought back to his conversations with Cassandra; he remembered that calmness seemed to be a recurring theme in their talks.

"It isn't meant to be alarming," Armand chuckled, "but it's actually meant to be a state of heightened awareness, intense focus."

Sam shifted his legs. Something in his pocket dug into this thigh, irritating him. He reached for it. It was his ball and cup game. Without thinking, he'd grabbed it as he got ready for the day. He withdrew it and looked over the toy.

It was a game, he understood that. But it was also someone else's creation, and while he appreciated that, he was now mindful of just how much of a distraction it had become. It had served a purpose, but that was before he'd come into the greatest understanding to his life thus far. He wanted to create something now.

He stood up, and threw the toy as far as he could. The two men watched as it rotated in a ragged, whirling arc, a topsy-turvy ballerina, and fell just past the rocks into the sea.

"I learned to meditate from my teacher," Armand said, "he was not wickie but a watchmaker. Who better to understand the value and meaning of time than the person who builds its measuring device?"

"I can't imagine sitting still for more than five minutes."

"Then meditate for five minutes. That's a good start."

"But how do I quiet my mind?"

"You don't." Armand stated.

The old man explained how he meditated. He sat on a pillow in a comfortable seated position, with his back straight and his eyes closed, his hands palms-down on his knees. First, he said, he took his awareness to his breath; he wanted it slow and regular. Next, he became present. This was done by listening to his breath, listening to any sounds around him, even listening to and feeling the beating of his heart. He released his hold on his mind and thoughts and, with his five senses, took in the environment in which he found himself. From there, he pictured the energy of the universe pouring into the crown of his head, and going throughout his body. As this happened, he relayed, he used the energy to heal his body, his mind, and his soul. He repeated this process several times, imagining the energy of the universe enriching and empowering him. After several minutes of doing this, his body buzzing with energy, he would wish peace and blessings to everyone on the earth.

This step accomplished, he moved onto the second step; focusing his energy. To do this, he explained, he felt the energy in his legs, starting with the tips of his toes. One leg at a time, he "pulled" the energy from his toes into the heel, from the heel into the ankle, and all the way up into the thigh. From there, he would work the energy up his body, collecting it in the spine. He repeated the process with the other leg, then repeated the process two more times with his arms, gathering all the energy from his limbs into his spine. Once there, he would focus his thoughts on one thing for several minutes at a time. He would repeat this process, with the same focus, for seven days. If he wanted to focus on courage, he would think about times when he felt particularly courageous, how his breathing felt, how his mind and heart had been. He would imbue this sensation of courage into all the energy bundled into his spine, and then redistribute the energy across his body and into his limbs, spreading courage or whatever attribute or state he was focusing on into his entire being.

When he became distracted, when he felt his awareness wandering, he would gently pull it back to wherever he was in his practice. He didn't get frustrated, didn't get upset with himself. He would redirect his awareness until he completed his meditation which, he confided, sometimes lasted as long as forty-five minutes.

Sam listened intently, taking all of this in. He set aside his apprehension, set aside his fears. He knew what Armand was saying was coming from a place of love, but more importantly, it was coming from a place of experience. Of having traveled a path, and now wanting to impart the knowledge from that path, undoubtedly gained through trial and misstep, in a fraction of the time.

As Sam listened, another deeper understanding flooded his consciousness, staying with him the way an open shell on the shore holds water from that wave that just filled it.

What was life, if not guided by some focused driving force. It was a series of events, strewn across days, weeks, years, and even decades. Without focus, without principle and purpose, it was the adorning of learned habits onto the tree of a person's makeup without the sense of arrangement of a greater meaning. It was the accomplishment of deeds, of tasks and chores that might fulfill some smaller objective or set of objectives. At best, these deeds might sew together moments in time but, without orchestration to some higher, even daunting purpose, would lead to something less than a wholly fulfilled existence.

He accepted failure was not the end, but rather the process by which one eliminated possibilities on the path to success. That it was not something to be feared, but something to be embraced. More keenly, he sensed that while he was not someone who could meditate for three quarters of an hour at present, if he practiced regularly and purposefully, he would grow into the man who could. And that principle was true of anything in life; he would increase his skill at whatever he focused on through the process of repetition. True failure then, was quitting.

There was a shift in his perception, like the movement

of concepts and ideas that he'd felt at work inside his brain upon coming out of the lowlight room had settled. He believed. He believed he could be the architect of his life and, as architect, could build a life that was a magnificent castle or one that was a ramshackle hut. He could build something great, or something desultory. It all came down to where he directed his awareness; mindset. Feed negative thoughts, and your life will grow deep in shadows of negativity. You will find the bad in good moments. Gradually, you will paint a dreary world that you see as normal.

Feed positive thoughts, and your mind will find the opportunity in every occasion. Even in life's hardest moments, you can find a lesson. A blessing.

Sam believed he could create a life full of meaning and fulfillment, one that would enable him to grow and contribute, to love and to create. He could create things that would inspire or uplift other people. Maybe even just one person. But that would be enough. These things might be stories, they might be books. But he knew they were in him. And he would bring them to life.

His knowing went further. He accepted wholly the notion that this compass of the mind of which Armand spoke was a reliable tool with which to navigate life, a life of his choosing. He understood that through practice and dedication to meditation, he could use the compass to increase his powers of concentration and will, and how they manifested inside of him.

"I want to meditate now."

Armand laughed. "I won't stop you. But, like anything, you'll get better at it when you make it a habit. I sometimes meditate during the day, but always first thing in the morning. Every morning."

"The first thing? Even before you...?"

More laughter. "No. When natures calls, I answer. Then, meditation. It sets the focus for the day."

Sam stood up and walked to the railing. The sun was just above the horizon now. He felt like there was so much to be done. It was exhilarating.

"Then that's what I'll do."

Journal Entry: We become our habits. How we wake up. The thoughts we think as we start the day. Making or changing a habit isn't purely a function of time; it's a function of want. If we really want to change something, we will. If we have a big enough "why" we will shape our lives in pursuit of that why. The universe will shape our perception of the world in pursuit of that why.

The mind. Awareness. Concentration. Willpower. These are the instruments to master the mind.

CHAPTER TEN
THE SEA OF DREAMS

The mind is a tool, it is not meant to be where you live. The words stayed with Sam after Armand uttered them, prompting him to write them down, along with other revelations he'd had while on the island. *Spending too much time in your head is like trying to get underway without drawing in the anchor.* The past was a place to learn from, not a place to languish.

Over-thinking, over-analyzing had prevented him from taking action in the past. He saw that clearly, and recognized that, the more he thought about doing something, the less likely he was to do it. It was different than being obsessed over a thing, like the idea of intending to do something sometimes shut off the inclination to carry it out. Almost like telling himself, 'I am going to do this' tricked his brain into thinking the thing was done and as a result, deflated the impetus for carrying out the deed.

When he shared this with Armand, the old man mentioned that while it was true the mind could be tricked into thinking an act had already been completed, it could be fooled into thinking the same thing about an outcome. Visualizing the outcome in one's mind, he offered, tricked the brain into thinking the outcome had already happened, and doing this would start to shape a person's thoughts and deeds towards the realization of the outcome.

Sam found it curious and mysterious how tricking the brain in one sense might hinder him from doing something, while in another sense would enable him to shape his reality.

"Perhaps, this is the most important lesson I can offer you," Armand stated as the apprentice packed his clothes, "You must commit your emotions to what you want. If you are burning with desire for the things you want, you'll find a way to make them so. That is the only way to truly shape your destiny. Wanting something badly enough will guide you to find a way. If you don't want it enough, you'll find an excuse."

Sam nodded.

"Distractions will come," Armand continued, "Setbacks will happen. Don't get frustrated. Don't get upset. Failure is nothing more than the elimination of pathways toward success."

Captain Stenson would arrive that evening. Her ten-day delay had come and gone. Sam was ready to leave, which was not to say he had mastered his awareness or his mind. He and Armand agreed that he had the tools; now, he needed to create the habits. While it would have been possible for him to improve on these things and stay at the lighthouse, he wanted to be home. Needed to be. Something pulled him back. Something that he never saw clearly, but was always in his peripheral vision. Something emanating from the universe urged him to leave the island. The old man sensed it, didn't attempt to talk Sam out of it, and offered that the lighthouse was open to him anytime he wanted to visit.

The two men had finished lunch and finished with the day's maintenance around Black Eagle early. Armand left Sam alone to pack up his belongings.

Sam had been meditating every day for the last week and a half. The first day, he had woken thirty minutes earlier than normal and sat in a meditative state for a paltry five minutes at the foot of his bed. On the second day, he tried in the garden room. While it was still dark, he found the atmosphere within that room helped him focus. He went everyday thereafter. By this morning, he was up a full hour ahead of his usual routine and, after a quick dip in the chilly ocean water to stir his senses, had convinced Armand to begin their duties early.

His meditative practice was still under ten minutes in total, but he could sense his concentration was increasing.

Much like his body had grown tone in responding to the heavy lifting that was part of working in the lighthouse, he knew his mind had also been strengthened as he spent more time honing his focus and improving his force of will. Sometimes while meditating, he'd hear a gull outside, or something would creak somewhere in the lighthouse. The first few times this happened, his mind chased the sounds, speculating as to their origins. If it was a bird, he wondered what kind of bird, and whether or not he could identify it by its sound. A seagull's cry was very distinct, easily picked out. The same was true for a raven, he concluded, not that they had any of the black-winged visitors.

At some point, Sam would realize his awareness had drifted from his meditation, and he would pull it back. Over the course of the past ten days, he had started to feel a change. The noises still happened, and he would acknowledge them with his awareness. The distractions became shorter in duration, and he would more readily resume his meditative practice.

Sometimes, he would acknowledge the sound as something that occurred in the present moment, but felt his focus remained on wherever he was in his practice. It was like the distraction was registered and logged in some mental archive, to be examined at a later time and place if warranted.

He wanted to write, and had been doing so regularly after the day's work was done. He wrote of the sea, and of pirates exploring far off lands. He wrote of love and loss, of triumph and treachery. He wrote whatever came to mind, and loved every minute that he did.

Captain Stenson and her crew arrived in the Viaje with the sun still

hanging high in the afternoon sky, a result of the days growing longer.

Sam took note of her and her crew, appreciating how dutifully they went about their work. The afternoon was pleasant, the seas peaceful. He helped Armand load the trash, and carried some of the empty crates back to the ship for their return to the mainland.

When the supplies had been offloaded, Stenson came up to the ground floor to where Sam and Armand stood. Sam had his knapsack draped around one shoulder, with his duffel bag in his other hand.

She offered to take the bag, and he readily accepted her invitation. Her surprise revealed itself in a smile. She started to say something to Armand, stopped herself, and managed a nod before turning and heading back to her boat.

"She doesn't trust you." Sam said as they watched her head down the steps to the dock.

Armand shook his head. "It isn't that. She wants to

know why. Why I have chosen a life that, to her, doesn't make any sense."

"Why have you?"

"My life is devoted to helping people," the old man mused, grabbing his fishing pole from against the wall. "And I love what I do."

Sam waited for more. He watched the lighthouse keeper examine the fishing pole, scrutinizing the integrity of the rod, testing the strength of the line. His mind buzzed, and he saw that the old man was completely immersed in what he was doing. Saw how each movement was measured and precise, no wasted energy. He decided his host had said all he was going to say on the matter.

"Well, thank you." He extended his hand, and Armand shook it. "I will be back. One day."

Armand rested his fishing pole against the wall. He returned to Sam, taking the compass from around his neck. He placed it in the younger man's hands, cupping his hand over it.

"I know you will. And when you return, I will be here. Go now, boldly towards the dreams before you, and live a life fulfilled."

Armand turned away, collected his fishing pole and tackle, and walked out the door without looking back. Two gulls flew overhead, exchanging chattering calls back and forth.

Sam walked outside, catching sight of the birds as they flew south past the island. As he watched, one bird arced west, while the other kept flying straight away. He took a deep breath, and made his way down to the boat. Captain Stenson greeted him as he boarded, and he asked if he might stand with her in the pilothouse. She welcomed him, and suggested he could steer, if he wanted to, once they were away from the dock.

The Viaje pushed gracefully away from Black Eagle Island, and as the boat cleared the dock, Stenson opened up the throttle and turned into the afternoon sun, headed home. Sam glanced back at Black Eagle Lighthouse one last time. Armand was by the shore, casting his line into the sea. The young man smiled as, without looking up, the old man waved.

Sam turned back around, smiled at Stenson, and looked ahead to the beckoning waters before him.